INDIGENOUS HERITAGE

IN AFRICAN LITERATURE

Smith and Ce [ed.]

AFRICAN
Library of Critical Writing

INDIGENOUS HERITAGE - in African Literature
Smith and Ce (Ed.)

©African Library of Critical Writing
Print Edition
ISBN: 978-9-7837-0361-2

 All rights reserved, which include the rights of reproduction, storage in a retrieval system, or transmission in any form by any means whether electronic or recording except as provided by International copyright law.

For information address:
Progeny (Press) International
Attn: African Books Network
9 Handel Str.
AI EBS Nigeria WA
Email: handelbooks@yandex.com

Marketing and Distribution in the US, UK,
Europe, N. America (Canada),
and Commonwealth countries by
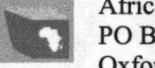 African Books Collective Ltd.
PO Box 721
Oxford OX1 9EN
United Kingdom
Email: orders@africanbookscollective.com

Contents

Contents	5
Introduction	7
Chapter 1	
Storytelling and Human Development	10
Chapter 2	
Female Bonding in Black Literature	25
Chapter 3	
Insigamigani (Heroic) Traditions	41
Chapter 4	
Rumuji Women's Dance	61
Chapter 5	
Time and the Traditional Palimpsest	74
Chapter 6	
Poetics of African Naming	88

Chapter 7

Proverbs in Ojaide's Contexts 112

Chapter 8

Igbo Traditional Morality 126

Chapter 9

Naming in Esanland 142

Chapter 10

Rhythms: in Honour of Achebe 155

Notes and Bibliography

Introduction

Indigenous Heritage in African Literature

WE can commonly agree with the assertion that the spirit of Africa as manifested in her great cultural forms which first spoke to the world through the art of Egypt speaks yet again to the contemporary age through the complex variety of modern black literatures. And while, as expressed through the medium of native tongues, it has been understood by only a small part of the world, yet through its complex interaction with other linguistic and cultural traditions Black has moved the world through her art.

Our previous series have witnessed to canonical and potential texts that adhere to the formula of African, and not Western, writing, whose characters attest to the survival of ancestral, ontological identities that can only point to an African literary antecedent. Recently too, there have emerged insightful perspectives into multiple temporal and spatial realities, and the state of the indigenous person in coeval space and time, where colonial grand and counter-narratives, et cetera, can all be processed together so that the interconnections and the understanding of indigeneity and its potential application for positive change could more clearly be seen in its fullest possible human ramifications. Thus the African novel in its very genre has proven to disembowel colonist, literary tendencies and philosophies and assumed for itself an independent position in the universe of world literature.

This edition commits to the depths of black identities in modern black texts. The cultural reclamation of an African origin and/or roots as tied to the solemn remembrance of the Ancestor has demanded the intense attention of enlightened black writers for the social and psychic revaluation of their generation and others that follow. It features a forum on the oral-written interface in Achebe's fictions, which reveals how folk materials revise the anthropological discourse of the West through which African cultures were inferioritized by juxtaposing an alternative idiom–of African orature–with its own unique manner of structuring reality that might offer a way of ending Africa's discursive indentureship to the West. The series further examines the dual status of the oral performer in African traditional societies which encouraged a wide range of human expression to create identity for members of the community Africa and proposes a challenge to sustain the methods of creative transmission through the continuing presence of these African performers who are living proofs of the survival of her oral traditions, especially in the propulsion of communicative action and the communicative strength of men, women and children in the community. It reiterates that European imperialism led to the most widespread disruption of communities in the world resulting in a society haunted by the loss of values and historical opportunities that could have held together the communities, and depicts how even the linguistic relationship in a novel could be manipulated to overcome the crisis of identity caused by the intruding foreign culture. It draws a nexus between the aesthetic of the novel and the social experience that nurtures the literary consciousness of the writer, showing how the fictionist imbues his art with a social vision that seeks to deconstruct elitist colonial apparatuses in favour of progressive ideals for socio-economic rebirth.

As we anchor the quest by writers from Africa and her Diaspora for enriching permutations in Black literary traditions in this volume, we hope that further research efforts continue the exploration of theoretical frameworks of propagating indigenous knowledge about the Black experience, discovering the tensions of space and identity at various political, social, economic and psychological levels of African national existence and their possible remediation through imaginative ideological fusions that are embedded in the external and subjective realities of our world.

Ce - Smith

Chapter 1

Storytelling and Human Development

O D Oamen

STORY telling has always been a product of human development initiated from the need to entertain, instruct, inform and educate the people towards a better society. Although the above need informs storytelling, it has been found to capture other aspects of life beyond its acclaimed tradition of a lullaby. These include politics, economics, health, social values and norms, with the social values being more appreciated than other areas. Our argument in this presentation is strengthened by a health related African development story entitled 'The Wise King.' It unveils the storyteller as a talented developer who uses the influence of the stage, environment, and language to relay an important message. The language of the storyteller is flexible, constructive and communicative. The developmental impact of African storytelling is evidenced by its recognition in cultural policy administration which recommends that African storytelling should be further studied with a view to exploiting its various useful components in broad ways for the purpose of development.

Storytelling as the product of human development started when civilisation began to make progress in interactions and thoughts about terrestrial and celestial existence. It evolved from the need to transfer values, norms, history, songs, poems et cetera, from memory to memory as there was no means of written records of human events. This was before the emergence of the art of symbolic representation which came before writing. Storytelling was useful for the storage of norms and values in its own time. Human memory was a good reservoir of experiences where they could easily be recalled, expressed or acted. Of course human memory has its own disadvantage, that is, when the person who is the reservoir dies, the reserve itself dies with him. Human civilisation realised this early enough and thus started the transfer of such storage from human memory to human memory through varying modes of expression, sometimes accompanied with songs. This is storytelling or folktale, the process of which has helped man's developmental process in recent times.

African Storytelling and Human Development

A lot of people understand only the traditional lullaby and entertainment aspects of African storytelling. These are the popular two segments covered by African storytelling that are readily appreciated. However, depending on the story, it covers other areas like politics, health, governance, religion and other aspects of development. From the beginnings of storytelling which is difficult to ascertain but assumed to be when man began to live in communities and interact with one another and the immediate environment, the essence of storytelling has been to preach morality. Morality constitutes the foundation of development. This moral essence of African storytelling is related all aspects of development, considering Rodney's view on development as a stage of growth or advancement of a human being or thing:

Development in human society is a many-sided progress. At the level of the individual, it implies increase in skill and capacity, greater freedom, creativity, self discipline, responsibility and material wellbeing. Some of these are virtually moral categories and are difficult to evaluate depending as they do on the age in which one lives, one's class origin, and one's personnel cadre of what is right and what is wrong. (1)

Rodney's definition cuts across several aspects of development, further stating that some of these are virtually moral categories which are difficult to evaluate. Yet the contribution of storytelling to development lies within the moral category. Storytelling is didactic; any aspect of human endeavour that is didactic is evaluable depending on the mode of evaluation. In as much as storytelling has a purpose, the achievement of that purpose could be used to evaluate it. One of the purposes of storytelling is to impact acceptable values and norms that project simple moral or ethical education. At this dimension of storytelling, emphasis is consistently placed on man and his relationship with his neighbours; when this relationship is healthy it becomes instrumental to the growth of a harmonious society (Oamen 128).

As an instrument for moral advancement, storytelling becomes a communicative art. As relevant as any human profession or business may be, e.g. law, medicine, pharmacy, politics, administration, etc, the individual is first a human, birthed by parents, from a society whose norms and values are wrapped in different cultural expressions. Storytelling is one of them and it has the power to impart acceptable moral values that will enable an individual to function in a given society and beyond. The ability of an individual to function with his personal and professional conduct in society forms a reasonable base to evaluate the impact of storytelling on his culture. African storytelling contributes to development through moral or ethnic bracing of members of the society. This in turn guides society's habits, especially with their neighbours either in their individual or professional conduct. As the 'The Wise King' exemplifies, African stories ensure their developmental purpose in relation to societal issues and needs.

'The Wise King'

Elo was the king of Azun. He died due to epidemic outbreak in the kingdom. After his death, his eldest son, Aza, took over his throne. Aza knew very well that his father died due to the epidemic outbreak in his kingdom. His father was not the only person who was affected. Many other people in the community also died. As a wise King, Aza took a decision with his council of chiefs to improve the sanitary condition of his community. Before he became king, the sanitary habit of the people was very poor. At that time, the entire people of Azun used one empty piece of land at the back of the village hall as toilet. Aza was not satisfied with this, therefore, he ordered every family head to organize his family and dig a pit. The king gave an order that nobody should defecate behind the town hall. Anybody found violating this order after a given time shall receive twelve lashes of horse whip on the back. So every family in the community came together and dug latrines for their families, while the king's was dug by the entire community.

One morning the king's mother was caught by watchmen posted around the town hall. She was taken to the king's palace. Everybody heard that the king's mother was caught defecating at the prohibited place. The entire community was eager to know how the new king will judge the case being the first crucial case he would handle. It was an opportunity for him to prove his wisdom.

As it was in the custom of the people, a day was set aside for the whip bearer to flog the king's mother in public. On the appointed day, the king took his mother to the venue where she will receive twelve lashes of the horse whip. Most of his subjects had thought that the king would waive the punishment binding on his mother but the king made up his mind to prove to his people that he was a king who believed in justice and equity.

Soon the whip bearer appeared and the king ordered him to give his mother twelve lashes of horse whip specified for the offender. As the whip bearer gave her the first stroke, the king's mother screamed and fell down. When the king saw her mother in agony, he stepped forward, disrobed himself and told the whip bearer to give him the remaining eleven strokes on his back. The whip bearer was scared but the king encouraged him to do his job and he did. The entire community was thoroughly frightened as there never had been a king like this in the entire kingdom.... (Oamen 4-6)

The above story has political and health implications on development as the king of Azun died from epidemic outbreak, probably cholera or malaria diseases, influenced by environment. His son took over and changed the sanitary condition in the entire community to avoid future recurrence. If the late king had exercised his authority over his people, he would have been able to notice their poor sanitary habit and probably may not have died from the pandemic. Because he was king, his death, however, brought changes. This is indeed a reflection of our modern societal experience: A dangerous pot hole in the middle of a highway will never be repaired until a prominent politician is involved in an accident and dies on that spot. Just like the death of king Elo, which awakened the son who passed a decree to improve the sanitary condition of the people, so also are state administrators only roused by tragic accidents, massive deaths and loss of property due to their own negligence in public responsibility. They are alerted only at the instance of an occurrence; thereafter, their usual complacency sets in.

We can deduce from the above story that people may have died in great numbers but nothing happened until the king became a victim. What is important, however, is that the sanitary condition of the people has undergone improvement. The success of the king's law was dependent on the action he took about the queen mother of the community who was the first violator. By public expectation, the king was expected to defend his mother but he allowed his mother to experience the pain and humiliation of violating a law made by the king by encouraging the whip-bearer to flog her just once. Then the king disrobed himself and took the remaining eleven strokes of the whip. This must have sent serious signals to his entire subjects that no one is above the law. It also indicated the premium place of sanitation in the health needs of the kingdom.

In modern political style of African administration, the king must be foolish not to defend the queen mother. But if he had defended his mother, he would have violated the spirit of the law himself had made. This would fulfil an African proverb which says: 'when a woman who owns a bowl would not value it, another woman will use it to pack refuse.' In essence, nobody would respect the king's decree and anyone could violate it just because the king and his mother had abused the law. The only means to remedy the situation was the bold action the king took against his own mother, otherwise the people could as well continue to defecate behind the hall and the pandemic could as well persist. The king's value placement enabled him to take a decisive decision that would alter old negative habits and enforce the ideal that will improve the health practice of the people, thereby enhancing development within the health system. The king took his action based on good sense of moral judgment. This, no doubt, strengthened his personality and authority as a king in his kingdom. In essence, he distinguished himself for respect and obedience from the people. Having taken a gallant action against his mother and himself, no reasonable citizen would decide to violate any of the laws.

The political implication of the story is that the king exercised his authority against himself and his mother with a view to improving the general health situation of the people. A process of proper health practice has been initiated, backed by authority, and influenced by development oriented moral values exemplified by the king for the good of the entire nation.

Development Values of Storytelling

African storytelling has been held in divergent opinions by scholars out of which a few schools of thought notably the entertainment, social functionality and literary aesthetic schools are prominent. Elechi Amadi propounds that literature is something meant to give pleasure to people, so if you concentrate too much on the vices in society and so on, you find the reader really gets bored and doesn't feel either elated or pleased (quoted in Emezue 344). But it was argued that people learn through facts of social relationships between man and his community, a child and his parents, a man and his relations and friends, and a man and his enemies (Egudu 35). Others proposed that the life of traditional oral literature is closely bound up with the life of man on our continent, with elaborate rites of passage, occupational interests, religious beliefs and social institutions (Epronti 77). Still the aesthetics of Chinweizu et al debate for the literary distinction of the story as a prose genre of orature in its own right. An analysis of an African story, like the one above, will reveal that each of these positions holds a value which contributes to development in society. African stories are related to every aspect of African life, depending on the situation. That means an African story as a communicative art must actually convey values for development in the process of telling it to the audience. The values communicated are not only relevant to its time but holds promises for the future. For instance, there are many African communities whose social systems fit into that of the story above. These are communities where people have never had public toilets, where they defecate about and endanger human life. Disseminated on a large scale, the above story is capable of reordering such communities' sanitary system. In practice, storytelling communicates values which are capable of enhancing development even in its entertainment and social functionality. The values communicated through storytelling would vary with or match many other aspects of human existence.

The Storyteller as a Developer

The storyteller is a communicative artist who explores his wealth of memory and a reservoir of oratorical traditions to the benefit of a ready audience, especially in less technologically sophisticated communities of past and present times. The storyteller reaffirms the usefulness of his story and the norms and values embedded in them in relation to his society or target audience. The storytellers in Africa have over the centuries used the resources of myriad languages to artistically affirm beliefs, values and social structures. In the process there has been much to celebrate and much to depreciate. The critic is to celebrate those values in storytelling that make greater inputs into our development, and depreciate those that will hamper development.

The storyteller is therefore a developer who utilizes the values in storytelling as moral blocks to build human minds for present and future advancement. The exploration of the nuances and patterns of his indigenous language by the storyteller artistically adds value, enhances expressive skills, and gives weight to his ideas. Sometimes he mimes and sings responsorial songs which involve every participant and, sometimes, the story is expressly performed in a drama. Often, in storytelling gatherings, questions are thrown at participants to measure their level of participation. This encourages each participant to listen attentively to every story till the end of the session which comes up every evening. At the end of each evening, participants would have learnt a story and a song, if any. Most importantly, they would have learnt the norms and values which have been deliberately built into the construction and communicative mechanisms of a story. Thus the storyteller, in this regard a builder, enhances the receptive ability of participants by telling and encouraging them to sit down and listen to morally sound and captivating stories as well as build their views through the responsorial songs which enhance their retentive ability as they learn and retain the stories and songs. The moral value input from the story, the trained voices, and the retentive ability of listeners that have been enhanced, are required for further education, skill acquisition or other related trade. All these contribute to the development of the society in various ways.

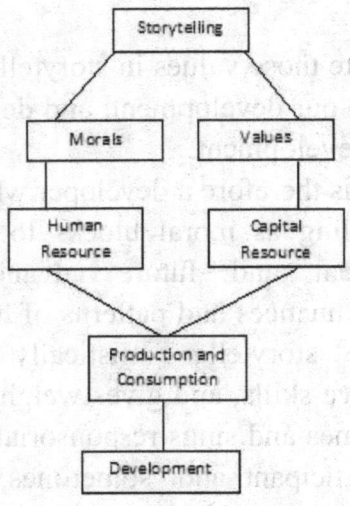

The above diagram shows that storytelling contains two vital moral and value elements. These are often seen as one but have their different functions as seen in the diagram. While storytelling informs morals and values, morals inform and build positive human resources, while values build positive and strong capital resources required for production and consumption. Effective production and consumption system enhances development. It is thus certain that any development which is moral and value based is more enduring and purposeful. It then becomes very important to build morals and values, through storytelling, because these are indices of higher civilisation and development. Morality and value have their extended usefulness beyond production and consumption. They go further deep to enhance human relationships. For instance, morality is required to live peacefully with others and is required as panacea for trust in any transaction. Retentive memory is needed for sound education or for skill acquisition. Voice is required for singing and other expressive skills. Each of these storytelling qualities is an aspect of development when exploited for economic purposes. This indicates that as the storyteller builds moral and mental aspects of being, he builds the society, by extension, and contributes to its development. There is no development without value placement. Mental, spiritual and material values are dependent on interpersonal relationships upon which every other human endeavour is dependent.

Stage and Environment in African Storytelling

The stage and environment employed by an African storyteller have developmental influence on his participants. Usually the stage round is used by the storyteller. The storyteller neither sits inside or outside the stage, rather he sits side by side with the participants in the round setting. The round in Africa symbolizes unity and strength. It means strength-to-strength because the sitting pattern is shoulder-to-shoulder, which is symbolic of the spirit of African communality. In West Africa the circle is an important element for any kind of theatrical action - it is a macrocosm symbolizing harmony, unity and communal experience (Rohmer 53). The circle reflects collectivism, and the space within represents the vacuum which exists in human mind, without knowledge. It is the vacuum which storytelling or any theatrical knowledge occupies. That is why the space is used for dancing, acting or singing. These are of developmental nature as everyone needs a place for support, which those in the circle are there to give. The spirit of brotherhood exists in the stage round and it is a collective representation of cooperation enabling people to work together in the society. Sometimes, for the purpose of familiarity, the storyteller weaves his story around his environment. This also helps him to deliver his message appropriately because his listeners are closer to the environment around which the story is woven. The environment helps the storyteller to infuse environment related problems about what is to be revered and what is not. This is aimed at his listeners who are supposed to know what is expected of them in terms of social responsibility, e.g., how to support a family and contribute towards the continuity, or the need for balance and stability in social, economic and political life. The stage and environment are important aspects of any story because they are the fabric in which the values and norms inherent in storytelling are presented and upheld.

In conclusion the relevance of African storytelling has made it responsive to the people's development needs even in the face of technological advancement and incursions of western civilisation. It then becomes necessary that storytelling as relevant and communicative art should be sustained as an art, a means of entertainment, for the moral impact that it is known for, as well as the amplification of its educative, informative and instructive content. Storytelling is basically dependent on expressive skills which enable it to appropriate language and environment to inform, educate and entertain with real vernacular effect, and with a view to developing man and enabling him to develop his society. This makes it necessary for stories to be studied and applied to areas of relevance. Most importantly, its lessons must be imbibed by young and old. Therefore, for storytelling to contribute more to development, it should be studied and introduced to the stage with closeness to reality as in drama.

The contribution of storytelling to the moral and intellectual development of African literature is obvious. It has impacted on Africans in terms of knowledge, honesty, diligence and intelligence. It has also enhanced social and cultural awareness of communities and their environment, improved expressive skills on the use of folk songs and their reordering to meet modern day challenges. The success of social, economic, political and technological development is dependent, at least in part, on morality, intelligence and good social behaviour which storytelling promises by helping to redirect the way we do things. It must be understood that storytelling has far developmental implications than ordinary entertainment and lullaby. As a means through which cultural policy implementation is explicated, the relationship between storytelling and development is an import which has yet to be fully acknowledged in cultural management. For instance, the Nigerian cultural policy states: 'the state shall preserve and present oral tradition, folklore… and popularise them by producing them in Nigeria' (quoted in Aig-Imoukhuede 171). To popularise and produce folklore through any media is a process of management. This process is important because of the usefulness of folklore to human existence especially in Africa. According to Nketia,

African societies attach a great deal of importance to these traditions because particular forms serve as medium for the expression of individual and group sentiments and thoughts as well as repositories of history and traditions, while also serving, as in other culture, simply as creative expressions that may be enjoyed in their own right in recreational, ritual, or ceremonial contexts. (1)

The richness of African folklore has endeared it to quite a few African writers led by Chinua Achebe who enjoy its aesthetic sources and seek to enhance its high creative imagination upon the reading populace. This is an example of how the folklore of a people is exploited for their developmental essence. The achievement of this development will be enhanced by a cultural policy which understands the need for folklore discharge and management in the developmental concerns of the continent.

Chapter 2

Female Bonding in Black Literature

A Kumar and S Jha

IN the short period of time since Gloria Naylor published her first novel, *The Women of Brewster Place* (1982) she has established herself as a self-avowed feminist and black cultural nationalist. Through the six novels which include *Linden Hills* (1985), *Mama Day* (1988), *Bailey's Cafe* (1992), *The Men of Brewster Place* (1998), and *1996* (2005), she joins a wide assortment of earlier writers—Shakespeare, Dante, Zora Neale Hurston and Toni Morrison—in a dialogue on the authentic representations of human condition. In *The Women of Brewster Place,* Naylor creates for herself an image of liberated black woman who gets ardent support from her black female compatriots. The novel consists of seven interrelated tales of the dispossessed women who all end up in Brewster Place. Each woman, in her own way, plays an important role in the making of Brewster Place. They are proud of their African roots and heritage, and are ready to face hardships for the betterment of their own people. The weather adds heavily to the bleak surroundings of the dead-end street that encases Brewster Place. In nearly every scene, there is a darkening sky hanging heavy over the blind street where the stories of seven women converge. Living in a world that has never been kind to them, they develop a sense of bonding among themselves that proves the only reason for their survival in this street. This bond could be understood as a mutual, supportive feeling of attachment and loyalty to one another, which grows out of a shared experience of oppression. It is this sense of female-bonding that enables them to deal with the everyday pressures they face in the male dominated society in which they live. "Only by forming bonds among themselves do the women overcome life's difficulties and find the necessary strength to survive in a changing world" (Montgomery 89). Whitt also comments on their self-dependent nature as "sassiness ...with an assurance that does not depend on male approval, that functions confidently on its own terms" (24).

Female bonding, as Dill notes, "has been a binding force in the struggle against male chauvinism and patriarchy" (131). In *The Women of Brewster Place* Naylor seems to tackle what Bell Hooks says is ingrained in the society: "We are taught that women are 'natural' enemies, that solidarity will never exist between us because we cannot, should not, and do not bond with one another" (127). This is quite evident from the fact that every woman in Brewster Place faces one or the other kind of obstacle which she overcomes with the help of the women around her. Naylor's novel shows how race and gender have been responsible for confining women to the street, and how they overcome the crisis created by the society in general and by their own people in particular. The resilient character of the women in the novel is evinced through their narratives and their experiences that they share at Brewster Place.

Brought to the American continent as slaves in the 17th century, African women were deprived of every basic human right in order to serve the plantation economy of the American South. They have been the victims of the lowest possible pay, the worst kind of poverty, the least access to child care, and targets of all sorts of violence, including battering, rape and involuntary sterilization. They have been viewed as an object of sexual exploitation, and portrayed as over-sexed, women who were always available for instant sexual gratification. They have been given a number of stereotypical images which are deeply rooted in American slavery. They were derided as Mammy, Aunt Jemima, Matriarch, Sister, Black Bitch and Girl. These stereotypes have been disastrous to the social progress of the Black community. As Jewell puts it: "the privileged classes use these 'images and ideologies' to keep African American women on the periphery of society, consequently limiting their access to societal resources and institutions" (4). Bell Hooks in an interview with Tanya McKinnon has interrogated the way images are constructed to perpetuate and maintain sexism and racism arguing that the whole media was responsible for portraying her (symbolically all black women) "in a false and distorted light which is merely part of the overall mainstream mocking of both feminist thought and women's studies"(815).

Thus this stereotyping could be seen as a process of oppressive ideology with a number of signals used against these women to underestimate and marginalize them. Blackness became symbolic of negativity, a sign of ugliness, uncontrolled irrational behavior, and violent sexuality. All this was done to deliberately undermine or destroy their self-respect, love, dignity and pride in their race. As Kulkarni says

...the purpose predominantly behind such a distorting portrayal is to deny the victim his basic humanity, to drum the notions of inferiority in his cerebral system so that all atrocities inflicted could easily be justified. This ideological environment fractures the victim's psyche, causing serious self-doubt and self-hatred in his mind. (55)

A number of African American writers have reacted sharply against this power structure and portrayal. Claudia Lawrence in "African American Intergender Relationships: A Theoretical Exploration of Roles, Patriarchy, and Love" focuses on roles and the expression of intimacy within intergender relationships stressing how "concepts of patriarchy and love accompanied by the historical experiences of African Americans as a group have given significance to understanding how African American women and men express themselves within their relationships" (623-639). Challenging this dominant ideology, Naylor creates in her novel female characters with bonding between them who question the existing sexist oppressions "bound by a sense of community and sisterhood that enables them to deal with the everyday pressures they face in the male-dominated society in which they live" (Khay).

Unlike Naylor's *Mama Day* (1988) where the bond among the women exists on the basis of shared history, culture and familial roots, in *The Women of Brewster Place* the female-bonding is based on the idea of common sexist oppression. Naylor further emboldens these women to have faith in their culture, rituals and traditions; "so great is the wealth of our experience, culture, and ideas we have to share with one another. We can be sisters united by shared interests and beliefs, united in our struggle to end sexist oppression" (65). In fact these women have given an identity to Brewster Place. They have become the permanent hallmark of Brewster Place, sharing their experiences, laughing together, and criticizing one another. "They came, they went, grew up, and grew old beyond their years. Like an ebony phoenix, each in her own time and with her own season had a story" (5). Most of them have come to live there simply because they do not have anywhere else to go, while a few, like Kiswana, have come there by choice. "Each woman, in her own way, plays an integral part in the making of Brewster place. The women are forced to rely on each other when the world seems to shut them out" (Npag). When these women discover that the legitimized patriarchal social set up has denied them the due attention, "they turn inward, look to each other, and find strength" (Montgomery 96) in one another's company.

The women remain stranded here for two reasons: first, they are women, and, second, they are black. The wall in the Brewster Place symbolizes a racial and patriarchal artifact which checks the access of these women to the mainstream world. But, ironically, it becomes responsible for the bond between the women. As Henderson points out: "The wall, the image that separates its inhabitants from the city and each other becomes, in the end, a source of communal strength as each woman faces her own personal demons and forms a powerful cultural link ... to dismantle this wall one brick at a time." (1003)

Since the women living in Brewster Place belong to the most backward group of the United States populace, they have never been given any place in society, and consequently have never got a chance to speak publicly. But all this does not mean that these women do not have talents; their talents comes out in full shine in the tenants' meeting:

This was the first time in their lives that they felt someone was taking them seriously, so all of the would-be-if-they-could-be lawyers, politicians, and Broadway actors were taking advantage of this rare opportunity to display their talents. It didn't matter if they often repeated what had been said or if their monologues held no relevance to the issues; each one fought for the space to outshine the other. (139)

There are seven women who narrate their stories; each one unique in her own way. "Naylor traces out the intertwining lives of these women, beginning with the book's dominant presence, Mattie Michael" (Smith 268). It's Mattie who acts like a binding force among all the women and their narratives. Since the novel is centered on dispossessed women, Naylor seems to pay a tribute to the community of women, "of which Mattie is hub" (Whitt 24). Whitt goes further to call Mattie, "the willing surrogate mother for each of Brewster Place's woman in need" (52). Mattie's role is inevitable in Brewster Place as she is "the life force at Brewster Place", and "puts her dearly bought wisdom at their service, becoming mentor, mother, nurse, and confidante" (Smith 269).

Mattie is the only woman who enjoys everyone's respect and love by virtue of her helping and motherly love for others. She becomes a spokesperson of Brewster Place, and her voice "becomes the voice of righteousness" (Harris 120). She plays multiple roles at Brewster Place as "she is the voice of reason when other roomers want to take action against the lesbian couples. She is the source of comfort to Ciel after her daughter is electrocuted. She is the person to whom Etta Mae turns after she has her most recent sexual fling. Mattie gives up living her own life in order to help other people live theirs…People take her without ever asking what has brought her to Brewster Place and without considering whether or not she wants a life of her own. And she gives them what they need" (120). This is quite evident from Mattie's story that patriarchy governs the sexuality, and if someone tries to go beyond or defy the sexual norms of the society, he or she is looked down upon and faces severe punishment. In Mattie's case too, we find that she is pushed out of her loving father's house for controlling her sexuality, after "becoming sexually active and pregnant as a teenager" (119-120). The same thing happens with the two girls, Lorraine and Theresa who "have come to Brewster Place not because they are economically deprived but because they are socially scorned" (47) for controlling their sexuality. The patriarchal world wants them to channel their energy to the opposite sex. Mattie always sides herself with these girls because they share this commonality. And she supports them when the other women want to take action against them. She finds nothing wrong with the two girls loving each other, "Well, I've loved women, too. There was Miss Eva and Ciel, and even as ornery as you can get, I've loved you practically all my life." (141)

Mattie loves not only Theresa and Lorraine; in fact, she loves every woman who moves into her life, and in return she gets plenty of warmth and response. Even when she was at her father's house, she used to share her secrets with her mother, not with her father, even though her father was affectionate, caring, and concerned about her well-being. Her mother too aligns herself with her. This is indeed the reason that she did not tell her father the name of the fellow who raped Mattie. Her mother even goes beyond that when Mattie is beaten by her father; she picks the gun, and "wrapped the fingers around the trigger and pulled...the edge of the fire place exploded and sent flying bits of bricks into Mattie's back and cut up her father's face" (24). This is the beginning of Mattie's journey, quite certainly the result of the gender situation. The gender situation, along with racial discrimination, proves to be a lethal combination in her life, which pushes her towards Brewster Place. When Mattie walks out, with her son, in search of a safer accommodation, she discovers after countless attempts that "there was no need in wasting energy to climb to steps in the white neighborhoods that displayed the vacancies signs..." (30). It is because of her color that she could not get a house in the white neighborhood, and since she does not have a legal husband, she does not get accommodation at a black "respectable place" (30). At the end of the day, it is an old woman, the kind Miss Eva who "rescues her and her young son from the streets and offers them the warmth, comfort, and security they need" (Montgomery 90). Miss Eva is a woman whose story in the novel sets "a repeated pattern of concern, generosity, and love between and among women" (Branzburg 118). It is in this house that Mattie lives until her departure for Brewster Place. Though Mattie loses the care and love of her mother, she gets the alternative in Miss Eva. This mother-daughter relationship generates the bond between women more strongly. Gradually, both of them become part and parcel of each other's life. Whenever during the mock fight Miss Eva speaks of her death, Mattie becomes restless as she "did not want to imagine facing the loss of another mother" (39). Even on their first meeting, both of them start sharing with each other their experiences as if they have known each other for years:

Miss Eva unfolded her own life and secret exploits to Mattie, and without realizing she was being questioned, Mattie found herself talking about things that she had buried within her. The young black woman and the old yellow woman sat in the kitchen for hours, blending their lives so that what lay behind one and ahead of the other became indistinguishable (34).

The reason, perhaps, for the bond between these two women, is that both of them are subjected to patriarchy when they try to control their sexuality and act according to their own will. When Miss Eva tells Mattie the story of her life, it's almost the same as Mattie's:

Child, I know what you talkin' about. My daddy was just like that, too. I remember the night I ran off with my first husband, who was a singer. My daddy hunted us down for three months and then drug me home and kept me lock in my room for weeks with the windows all nailed up. But soon as he let me out, Virgil came back and got me, and we was off again. (34)

Mattie's bond with Miss Eva is not only a daughter-mother relationship; it is also that of a mentor, and a guide. There exists a friendship between Etta and Mattie too, which exhibits the powerful and preserving quality of female friendship. These two women have been friends since the days of their struggle and rely upon each other for their survival. Mattie and Etta discover a sisterly bond between themselves because of their common experiences, for both of them have experienced disappointment in love. It is natural that in each other's company they acquire the strength they need: "Etta laughed soft to herself as she climbed the steps towards the light, and love and the comfort that awaited her" (79). Etta knows that she may be disowned everywhere, but there is someone who is "waiting for her. It is Mattie who has always been constant and the comfort" (Whitt 32). Another commonality that both of them share is their final arrival. In spite of their moving in directions different, they have ultimately reached Brewster Place because of the existing racial and gender condition in American society which is not ready to accept their "blooming independence" (60). Mattie's presence invigorates in Etta with a deep sense of freedom and self-confidence. Both the women share everything that has happened in their lives. When Etta comes to Brewster place, they move "back, a singular turn that claimed co-knowledge of all the important events and almost all of the unimportant ones" (58). The bond between Etta and Mattie may be viewed as both sisterly and friendly.

So far as the bond between Mattie and Ciel is concerned, its roots are very deep, and it goes back to the time when both of them were happily living in Miss Eva's home. Though they belong to different generations, they rely upon each other. Ciel is portrayed as a child who looks at Mattie for knowledge and wisdom about how to handle situations in her life. She values Mattie's experience and often looks to her for motherly approval.

Serena's death comes as a blow in Ciel's life. She breaks down completely with pain and grief, and gives up the desire to live anymore. At this time when she is in such a critical condition and needs motherly care and support, Mattie moves with a strong impulse to protect her, "like a Black Brahman cow desperate to protect her young, she surged into the room, pushing the neighboring woman and others out of her way" (103). Her love for Ciel manifests itself when she brings Ciel literally back to life and persuades her to release the pain that she has been holding inside:

And she rocked...Ciel moaned. Mattie rocked. Propelled by the sound, Mattie rocked her out of bed, out of that room, into a blue vastness just underneath the sun and above time...She rocked her into childhood and let her see murdered dreams. And she rocked her back, back into the womb, to the nadir of her hurt, and they found it – a slight silver splinter, embedded just below the surface of the skin. And Mattie rocked and pulled–and the splinter gave way, but its roots were deep, gigantic, ragged and they tore up flesh with bits of fat and muscle tissue clinging to them. They left a huge hole, which has already starting to pus over, but Mattie was satisfied. It would heal. (103-104).

Mattie gives her a healing bath which breaks into tears in Ciel's eyes: "The tears were flowing so freely now Ciel could not see and she allowed herself to be led as if blind." (105) "And Ciel lay down and cried. But Mattie knew the tears would end. And she would sleep. And morning would come" (105). Mattie does all this in order to negate "the psychological destructive effects of temporality, the cycle that has led to the almost overwhelming tragedy Ciel now faces" (Montgomery 91).

Mattie has been quite successful in her life in establishing the bond with every woman who comes in touch with her. Only she stands with the women whenever they need her, and still she does not intrude in their personal lives. Cora Lee, for example, "sincerely likes Mattie because unlike others, Mattie never found the time to do jury duty on other people's lives" (123). Though Mattie is the central figure, there is, in the novel, one more woman who puts in her best effort to organize and unite the women of Brewster Place. She is none other than Kiswana Browne who has come to live at Brewster Place by choice, for she has a genuine desire to serve her people and assert her African identity. The purpose of her life, she claims, is to be "with my people, fighting for equality and a better community" (83). She is radical in her thought and approach and listens to nobody. She rebukes her own mother when she says that she is "trying to be what you're (she's) not" (85). She goes on to say: "trying to be something I am not, Mama! Trying to be proud of my heritage and the fact that I'm from African descent. ...I'd rather be dead than be like you—a white man's nigger who's ashamed of being black!"(85). This does not mean that these two women do not love each other. Her mother is concerned about her, for she encourages Kiswana not to be afraid of anybody, not even her mother. Further, she leaves seventy-five dollars for her when she leaves the house. Apart from all this, both of them agree on the point of the exploitation of black people in the United States, "a country still full of obstacles for black people to fight their way over—just because they're black" (84).

Kiswana Browne tries to bring all women of Brewster Place under the banner of Tenants' Association where they may come up with their problems and fight together for their cause. She knows that it is not an easy task, but she is not willing to give up. She does this as part of her agenda to fight "for equality and a better community" (83) for her own people. In this pursuit, she goes to Cora Lee whose life is falling apart because of her attitude towards herself and her children. Kiswana comes to her a as a breath of fresh air and kindles self-confidence in her by inviting her and her children to the black performance of *A Midsummer Night's Dream,* thus providing the aesthetic satisfaction to fill the vacuum in her life. This aesthetic satisfaction is quite evident from her action after the play gets over: "Cora applauded until her hands tingled, and felt a strange sense of emptiness now that it was over—Cora went down the row to Kiswana and grabbed her hands "thanks so much—it was wonderful" (126).

Through the play Kiswana brings some hope in her saturated life and compels her to rethink of her responsibilities for her children. It is for the first time that Cora realizes how much ragged the clothes of her children are, and she is surprised to see so many other incidents happen in her house. She resolves to check her children's home work every night, and send them to summer school. She does also repent as to why "she had beaten him (Sammy) for writing the rhymes on her bathroom walls" (127). She would now dream about her children in "good jobs in insurance companies and the post office, even doctors or lawyers" (125-126).

Kiswana knows well that though these women live at the same place, they are quite different in their ways and their perception of the society. This further complicates her problem of uniting them. There are a number of women who do not like the two girls—Loraine and Theresa, simply because they like each other. This bond of the two girls becomes an object of jealousy, not only for others, but also for their own people. This jealousy comes out when Sophie expresses that the two women should not be there because of their strange ways. It's Etta and Mattie who come to their rescue: "those two girls who mind their business and never have a harsh word to say 'bout anybody—them the two you mean, right, Sophie?" (140). When Sophie further argues that they are sinning against God, Etta rebukes her by saying that then the God Himself would take care of their sin and that He has not appointed her to scold them.

The debate, whether to include or to exclude these two girls who "at first seemed like such nice girls" to the association, leads to the brutal rape of Lorraine. Though late, the incident unites all the women of Brewster Place: "there is a vital oneness created among all the women of Brewster Place as a result of the vulnerability of black womanhood" (Montgomery 95). Every woman apprehends this kind of brutal rape, for Ciel had a dream about it, and something in it told her that she should be there as she is needed. Ciel even goes further to identify herself with Lorraine; she utters: "there was a woman who was supposed to be me, I guess. She didn't look exactly like me, but inside I felt it was me....And something bad had happened to me by the wall—I mean to her—something bad had happened to her" (179). Lorraine has been raped under the shadow of the wall which is a racial and patriarchal artifact so the women decide to uproot the wall from there. In Mattie's dream, all women contribute to bringing down the wall, smashing through the barrier that cuts them from possibilities: "Women flung themselves against the wall, chipping away at it with knives, plastic fork, spiked shoe heels, and even bare hands" (186). Dismantling the wall is a resistance against the male-centered, authoritarian and racist society, and is an expression of their composite strength.

Naylor's clear, yet often brash language creates images both believable and consistent. A reviewer in *Washington Post* notes that "Naylor is not afraid to grapple with life's big subjects: sex, birth, love, death, grief. Her women feel deeply, and she unflinchingly transcribes their emotions; Naylor's potency wells up from her language." Her story's seven main characters speak to one another with undisguised affection through their humor and even their insults. Naylor places her characters in situations that evoke strong feelings, and she succeeds in making her characters come alive with realistic emotions, actions, and words.

Chapter 3

Insigamigani (Heroic) Traditions

R Rwirahira

SMIRNOV Oleg views heroism as fitness cost to the individual via increased risk of death hence we might expect it to be eventually disappearing from the human population. Yet heroism certainly does happen with some frequency across a wide variety of cultures and societies (18). The term heroism itself had been narrowed down from warfare incidents to socio-welfare. Indeed Smirnov makes it clear on character traits which should define a hero in different circumstances, from which altruism or self sacrifice for a group community or a country can occur in warfare. He asserts that if heroism by definition is an altruistic response on behalf of one's group in the event of war with some other group, its task demands would appear prima facie quite distinct from those of other altruistic behaviors, for example, providing food to others and caring for the sick (18).

It is plausible that heroism could have evolved on its own trajectory, independent of other forms of altruism, and with warfare as the agent of selection. In this case associating heroism as a willingness to fight for one's group even when it places oneself at a reproductive disadvantage relative to other group members can evolve based on the selective pressures of war within a population or groups. A hero, however much can be narrowed down to include the five typical models, mainly divine, leader, common, ironic and romantic, as argued by Campbell Joseph, who noted that while Northrop Frye in his *"Anatomy of Criticism"* emphasized the cultural value of a particular quality made evident through archetypes, various mythologies suggest a common quest in which the individual is summoned from the familiar world, usually a hut or castle, to face a challenge; it is here that the hero encounters a "protective figure" who bestows the hero with some sort of power in a shape of weapon and amulet and thus the hero is well-armed for the task ahead (69).

The hero then proceeds to defeat an obstacle blocking progress of the adventure. The hero enters an unfamiliar world, a "dark kingdom," in which he or she is both tested and helped by various individuals; the hero then prevails through the tribulation and is rewarded, usually through marriage or fame, and in variations may have the reward stolen and then returns home. Campbell and Vladimir Propp share similar ideas on trends that a hero goes through. For example, Propp argues that the actions that fall into a hero's sphere include departure on a quest; reacting to the test of a donor; marrying a princess, and so on and so forth.

However Northrop Frye presents a particular heroic model based on archetypes of common imagery in Western literature, in various contexts to include Classic and Christianity. He distinguishes some five different models of a hero as (a) the divine hero, who is superior in kind to both humans and a normal human atmosphere; (b) the romantic hero who is superior in degree to normal humans and typical human situations, where laws of nature are slightly suspended, but is human nonetheless; (c) the leader-hero, who while superior in degree to other humans and more intelligent and virtuous, is still limited by normal human surroundings; (d) the common-hero who, as implied by the name, is on the same level of an average human and her surroundings; and (d) the ironic hero or anti-hero, who is inferior in skill, intellect, power, or possibly even moral character to the average human, yet exists in a normal human atmosphere; and while this kind of hero lacks qualities that are typically understood as heroic, he or she still manages to achieve heroic actions (143-145).

Heroism in Rwandan Mythology

The mythology in Rwanda acknowledges the courage and heroism that had been a paramount character trait among Rwandese mainly in the pre-colonial era. Different kings in their respective reigns had so projected to extend Rwanda to far reaching edges that would it be that borders had to be drawn and an end put to ancestral warfare some people believe Rwanda would have been an enormous nation in Africa.

The determination in self sacrifice makes Rwandese an exceptional people in the whole region. Rutayisire Paul, et.al argues that the king Ruganzu Bwimba and his sister Robwa had shown an outstanding heroic love to Rwanda until they died for it. This was demonstrated during the first battle between Rwanda and Gisaka overtaken by Rwandese later (16). Other kings who followed the paths of Rugwe and his sister to further extend the country preserved highly the integrity and identity of Rwanda amid the neighboring countries. Rutayisire argues that it was a respected country amongst others.

Heroism in Rwanda became a way of life to some extent because people were driven by nothing but conquest to further extend the country, and they were too much exposed to various war and conflicts. Rutayisirte singles different kings who expanded widely the country, among them Ruganzu Ndoli, who was taken as a demigod and an outstanding warrior that Rwanda had ever known. He writes that Ndori revived Rwanda, a country which was in the hand of Abanyabungo, and a lot of things were named after him. He blended the new kingdom's emblem Karinga, after Abashi took over Rwoga the first emblem. Ruganzu fought and defeated Bunyabungo and Bugara communities as a revenge for his country, he got Bunyambiriri, Bwanamukari, and Bugoyi, Byahi, Bwishya and Bufumbira in the volcano region (17). According to Rutayisire the country was formally structured having the king, the queen's mother, elders and fighters as the top decision makers. The king was mandated to distribute the power and was the only custodian of the monarchy emblem Karinga. He represented God and was a demigod (18).

Heroism in Rwanda cannot be narrowed down to reflect the pre-colonial era alone, it was a culture and a legacy from the ancestors that continued to flourish during the colonization and after independence. Two categories of heroes mainly Imanzi and Imena have now been given a memorial day in the whole country. The acknowledgement of seven people to include those in the colonial era, 1994 genocide and liberation war are still honored for their heroic performances in preserving, fighting and dying for the country's well being.

In Imanzi category, we have the late major general Fred Gisa Rwigema, who died in the 1990 liberation war that saved the lives of different Rwandese people. In the same category we also have the common Unknown Soldier who also died during the same war. The Unknown Soldier is a representation of every soldier who died fighting for the country to be liberated from the hands of genocide perpetrators in 1994.

Under the Imena category we have, the king Mutara Rudahigwa, the son of Yuhi Musinga who died mysteriously after he was taken by Belgians. He was said to be a strong pacific patriot, who despite his cooperation with the Belgian protectorate, wanted to see his country and people free from the hands of white people. There is also Michelle Rwagasana who was his close aid and might have died in the same circumstances.

Lastly, the country also honors and remembers the three late genocide heroes who died trying to protect others for being killed. Those include Agatha Uwiringiyimana, who was the Prime Minister in 1994, Felcite Niyitegeka a then parish administrator and Nyange students; they all died because of what their ethnic identities and what they believed was moral and genuine for Rwandese citizen.

Heroic Models in Rwandese Insigamigani texts

Rwandese Insigamigani texts are rich and have treated largely the idea of heroism alongside patriotism, with regard to how people might have lived within a certain timeline. Using the heroic models as defined by Northrop Frye to different proverb subjects (Insigamigani) and their different heroic performances during fighting, protecting and representing Rwanda positively, we have -

(a) Divine heroism

According to Northrop Frye the divine heroism is beyond and involves actions which are said to be beyond human capacity and imagination. In fact a Divine Hero, is a person who is "superior in kind" to both humans and a normal human atmosphere. It is very easy among Christian believers to associate Jesus as a divine hero as it is believed he gave up his life for the whole world to be saved; he belonged to heaven and earth at the same time (143). Divine heroism has mainly been seen in the Insigamigani proverb "He is not a man, but a strong tree".

In the proverb *"He is not a man, but a strong tree"* the narrator depicts Ruganzu Ndoli as a superhuman character - some Rwandese up to now believe Ruganzu was a demigod. The Ruganzu Ndoli was a son of Ndahiro Cyamatare killed by Abakongoro from the current Uganda, and Rwanda as a country vanished for 11 years. Ruganzu who had exiled in Tanzania as a child came back in Rwanda as a savior; he revived the country after all those years. The tasks he faced in the same process of reviving the country, were tough and had to be done by none other than a superhuman character, the King Ruganzu Ndoli who in this context can be labeled a divine hero. His strategy of spying and hitting back both as king and as warrior made him extend the country to reach the far horizons. Ruganzu started to fight alone using different spying and mendacious strategies to recover the whole country from the then occupant tyrants. He is believed to be divine because of his supernatural power which he used while fighting from the eastern parts of the country going to the west until reaching the Kivu lakes. The narrator recites:

One day, Mukire came to visit Ruganzu at his house, and Ruganzu saw him appearing in the yards, he went and pretended to sleep and covered himself with heavy metal objects. Mukire asked to see him and was told that he was asleep and could only be awakened by a hit of an axe on his chest. Mukire took an axe and hit him hard, Ruganzu could not be touched or feel the hit of an axe because he had covered himself with heavy metal objects, he only felt a slight knock. "Who is that waking me up?" Ruganzu mumbled while waking up. "It is me your master Mukire," Mukire responded. Ruganzu woke up and they had a talk, Mukire went back home after the conversation. *He is not a man, but a strong tree.* (114)

(b) Leader heroism

The Leader-hero is a person while superior in degree intelligent, virtuous, is still limited by normal human surroundings. As far as these proverbial narratives are concerned such person will be compared to kings. Kings in Rwanda were demigods as Rutayisire earlier asserts; this confirms why they are still limited to normal human beings and surroundings. Indeed they had to be intelligent and virtuous, since it was cultural and obvious to undergo typical different royal education; they were taught how to behave virtually and majestically if they were to lead the country. However, some of them went very far and became heroes. The narrator here has talked about two related kings, Mibambwe Sekarongoro Mutabazi and Ruganzu Bwimba who showed various heroic performances when fighting for the country either to expand it or to retake back some of its parts which were in the hand of the enemies. Hence the main proverbs where this heroic model is largely used: *"Keep your food, if you don't know the story at Fumbwe"* and *"He reaches Yihande horizons"*.

In the first proverb *"Keep your food, if you don't know the story at Fumbwe"* the narrator descriptively recites how Mibambwe Sekarongoro Mutabazi started to fight for his country from when he was young:

The first time Abanyoro fought with Rwanda, they were defeated and went back home. It was under Kigeli Mukobanya and it is said that his son Sekarongoro Mutabazi did earn the royal name of Mibambwe because of his brave services during the war from which he got seriously injured at the frontline. Keep your food, if you don't know the story at Fumbwe. (125)

In the second proverb *"He reaches Yihande horizons"* the narrator recounts a story of how Ruganzu Bwimba who was the king of Rwanda, from 1312 to 1345, died fighting offensively, in the then Gisaka dynasty:

Nkurukumbi was an uncle to Ruganzu Bwimba, another Rwandese king who reined in between 1312-1345, the king himself is well known for his royal martial services, in Gisaka dynasty and Bucengeri in the current Ngoma district, where he died. After Nkurukumbi suspected an underhand attack from Gisaka dynasty to

Rwanda, the king had no other choice but to suddenly attack and fight first, he went to fight without observing war initial rituals, which were to ask gods protections. He reaches Yihande horizons. (19)

The Symbolism and Imagery of Insigamigani Texts

Rwandese Insigamigani narratives are rich with symbolism, dialogue, imagery and hyperbole as extensive literary features. These Insigamigani texts are first proverbs and they became narratives when the authors trace the origins of the respective proverbs and then draw a plot of the whole story. As we illustrated earlier, proverbs here stand for popular sayings that contain advice and state generally the accepted truth; Insigamigani refers to subjects (people, objects, animals, etc.) from which different proverbs have originated. Thus Insigamigani texts are stories embedded in proverbial and narrative forms.

Bussmann argues that the words symbol and symbolism are derived from the Greek word meaning "to throw together." A symbol creates a direct, meaningful equation between a specific object, scene, character, or action and ideas, values, persons, or ways of life. If effect, a symbol is a substitute for the elements being signified, much as a flag stands for the ideals of a nation. In the proverb "*What is followed by men is finally reached*", the narrator talks about three main symbols and imageries at the same time: Men, the Buffalo and the Horns. To begin with, the narrator introduces the proverb by saying that it is uttered in a situation when people opt to work on a difficult decision. You hear others saying: *"What is followed by men is finally attained.* Men in this context are symbolic since they represent the whole society, as he argues. With the word 'people', the narrator is not being chauvinistic in order to minimize the whole society to nobody else but men. In this case men as another extra image by the narrator represent the people in a given area or circumstances. He uses this to deliberately communicate that when there is an emerging issue people should go for it. Regardless of how threatening it can be, people (women and men) should act altruistically to overcome it.

The Buffalo is symbolic, in a way that the narrator depicts it as a serious common threat, it becomes imagery because it can be seen as a predator in the society and has to be dealt with. Its presence out of the forests was a situation which required serious measures and decisions. The narrator evokes again the sounds of horns which are symbolic in a sense that they were communicating to the people and the forests, the death of a giant animal; horns turn out to be imagery since they represent an alarm device that makes a loud warning sound, although, apart from being a signal, the horns might stand for achievements of hard work done by the people.

The proverb, *"Rumors ended up in Gishike"* identifies the symbols, Gishike, as a place, and Rumour as a situation. In the proverb, *"He reaches Yihande horizons"* Yihande horizon stands for a place of no life, a desert and a land of no help. In the proverb *"Words or things have attained Ndabaga's phase"* the narrator uses both symbolic places and characters to convey the meaning of the proverb. He introduces the narrative by saying that such proverb is uttered when things turn to be impossible or socially unbearable, if not to say extremely difficult. There is a belief about its origin, but people don't talk about the real source of the Ndabaga's character. Thus Ndabaga and her father Nyamutezi are symbols as far as this narrative is concerned; the battle camps and the training camps are also spatial symbols.

In the proverb, *"Not everything fine is entirely perfect"*, the narrator, brings to mind the reader that this proverb should be uttered in a situation where a delightful moment gets interrupted by undesirable circumstances, and because of that there will be no complete happiness. As the narrator recites:

"Look we have few cows, and your wife is not meant for our family, what if I get married and you gave out cows. There will be a shortage of milk, and Kalira would not get sufficient milk, consequently, she will grow thin, and the people will start to gossip around that we were given a wife; we couldn't manage to care of, there are possibilities for her to be taken from us, in case we fail. Therefore, I would suggest not to marry soon, so that we can be able to take care of Kalira accordingly, the time, we will have a sufficient number of cows, I can get married and you can give me cows," the younger brother suggested. They all agreed on the decision. *"Not everything fine is entirely perfect."* (92-99)

Symbolism as a multiple style in these meta-genres can again be seen in the proverb *"Measure your beehive to Bugegera's one."* In this proverb we are again drawn to another appeasing story of how to achieve great social success out of goodwill and good intentions. In fact, the narrator explains that this proverb is uttered when people want to teach others to adopt good and moral behaviors from some ideal people. Bugegera as a name is allegoric and symbolic at the same time. Literally, the name might be associated to 'Kugegera' a Rwandese verb which means to be redundant or to be an idler, a person who has nothing and has nowhere to go. Much as Bugegera in this context represents a minority group in the society, this does not necessary makes him an idler. He was a servant, although the narrator says he was very poor and had disabilities: "Even if Bugegera was a servant, he was said to be poor, and he was physically deformed, he didn't have fingers on his right palm. *Measure your beehive to Bugegera's one*" (58). Although Bugegera is poor and malformed, physically, but his head is intact and can generate good ideas to get him out of poverty. In this regard, Bugegera is symbolic in the sense of courage and commitment; this is shown when he told his wife to brew a very tasty banana wine, for everyone who would help him to fix a beehive for honey. The narrator recites:

She brewed a very tasty wine, call it a render speechless wine; so many people came in to have a sip. Bugegera took advantage and announced to his visitors his intention. "Listen to all of you people gathered here, I would wish to offer an extra tasty wine to any person who would make a beehive for me," he asserted. *Measure your beehive to Bugegera's one*. (58)

In our last proverb "*The venue is at Huro*", the speaker reminds us that such proverb is only uttered when people signal to each other on the agreed decisions or places of meetings. To clearly explain the same proverb the narrator in his story talks about Huro and the forest (imagery) as a symbolic places plus Muberamfura a symbolic character. Huro as an agreed place for the last meeting is symbolic in the sense that it stands for serenity, a place of peace and justice. It is after the two related brother Murego and Rugango reached there after a long journey of insecurity, they managed to be at ease and got their lives saved and secured. The narrator recites:

I have a brother Mugenza who live at Huro in Bumbogo, he is a very good servant to Mibambwe Gisanura, if I manage to get you to him, you will be in good hands and he can recommend you to serve Mibambwe, who in return can ease your cases," he told the brothers. *The venue is at Huro.* (67, 69)

The forest imagery represents darkness, a closure of a death, and in this context it has been used as short time place of a refuge. Since the brothers were being hunted to be executed, Muberamfura who was living in the same forest appeased their worries and let them stay with him for a while. The same forest stands for a transitional unsafe place to be. The main idea was to take the brothers somewhere safe and that would be at Huro.

Lakoff and Johnson note that the common denominator of all metaphors is that one domain of experience that is less structured in a relevant respect is understood in terms of another domain that is more well-structured in the same respect. They argue that simply, one thing is thought of in terms of another. The function of metaphoric predications runs the scale from epistemic to expository.

In other words, it is used to think things that would otherwise be difficult to think at all, to give a better illustration of an idea that would otherwise be more opaque, or just to find a catchy way of framing a pre-existing idea. (15)

In Insigamigani text, narrators rely on historical objects, names, situations and incidents to give a clear explanation or a picture in a reader's mind. It is throughout the proverbial narratives that we are able to differentiate symbols and metaphors, simply because metaphors may be unconsciously depicted. Symbols can be used deliberately, since the author may want to stylize his artifact to meet different purposes. However, as again Lakoff et. al asserts, metaphors might occur even if the author or the narrator did not think about them. They can later be identified by him or the reader. In the same Insigamigani texts not all proverbial narrative carries metaphors; there are only five Insigamigani texts that have used remarkably metaphors. In this section we are going to use the above insights and ideas on metaphors to illustrate the logic behind them.

For a start we can identify the use of metaphors in the proverb *"Not everything fine is entirely perfect."* In the same proverb the speaker puts some few names and one place to point to the reader's mind a relationship of evidences to the depicted incidents. He talks about King Yuhi Mazimpaka and his daughter in law Kalira who later was nicknamed Rwabami and a place called Kivumu cya Mpushi as metaphoric features in the narrative:

"That is injustice and hostility, you need to give back that husband's wife," the king urged him. ... The king asked the husband whether he cannot accept another wife, be it from the house or any other place. ..."No one amongst you deserves this wife other than the king himself, from now onwards she is mine," the king affirmed. Not everything fine is entirely perfect. (92-99)

Another metaphoric usage can be identified on the nickname Kalira was given (Rwabami) by the people as the narrator recounts, "Kalira was nicknamed Rwabami because she became a wife to two kings-Yuhi Mpazimaka and Cyirima Rujugira. *Not everything fine is entirely perfect"* (92-99). A reader or a hearer can easily associate the name Rwabami, which literally might stand for a property of two kings, to Kalira who became a wife of the two kings in different circumstances. She was married to Rujugira but his father who was also a king by force made her his wife for some time. Kalira as a wife was subjected to every possible condition. The metaphoric feature is that of a place which the narrator calls Kivumu cya Mpushi. He speaks of a skin disease that Kalira suffered at that place while trying to make her husband come back from an exile. The place is metaphoric in the sense that it entails two pictures, a tree and a disease: Kivumu is a renowned resistant tree in Rwanda which is said to be huge and contains liquid bitter substances in a form of milk. Mpushi is a delivered name from a skin disease Ibihushi from which symptoms its patient scratches the body too much until it twists. Hence, a reader who sees all these pictures can understand why that place came to be named so. Because there was a Muvumu tree and Kalira stayed there while she was suffering that severe skin disease.

The proverb where a metaphor has been identified as the name of a person who killed the legendary king Ruganzu Ndoli, a certain Bitibibisi is *"He is not a man, but a strong tree."* This proverb should have been called *"He is not a man, but Bitibibisi"* but for translation purposes we have chosen to replace Bitibibisi to a strong man, not because it is the appropriate term to use but because proverbs are dynamic and relative and to some extent should communicate flexibly. Nevertheless the name Bitibibisi, its meaning would be close to the fact of being strong, something which is strong is also exceptional and unique.

The Ethic of Insigamigani Texts

Primoratz Igor posits that there is a major tradition in moral philosophy which understands morality as essentially universal and impartial, and seems to rule out local, partial attachment and loyalty. The center of morality to him is when love of one's own country characteristically goes together with dislike of and hostility towards other countries. Drisko associates morality as determination to work for the better of one's country. He asserts that citizens in order to be effective need to act from respect for the common good. They need to be willing to deliberate about the nature of the public good and how to achieve it. They also need to possess compassion, ethical commitment, social responsibility, a sense of interdependence among people and between people and their environment (110). Miller Richard concurs with Drisko by saying that commitment to these principles expresses the desire to be worthy of the trust of all those who respect one's own autonomy while insisting on respect for their own autonomy. No doubt, much more is required for the height of virtue. He expresses it better by saying that overriding desire of this kind at least makes someone a morally responsible person, a person who avoids wrongdoing if her acts are faithful to her goals (169). The above insights on morality as far as the country is concerned are far-fetched and cannot be limited to the obvious virtual aspects, to include respect, will, love and care or any other typical positive code of conduct to observe as a citizen. However, to add to the former aspects of morality, the insights are likely to relate, if not to say completely related and extensively manifested to Insigamigani narratives.

Referring to the proverbial narratives, we intend to pull out various positive behaviors and intentions that might have depicted by the authors. For example in the proverb *"What is followed by men is finally attained"* readers are being advised on the idea of solidarity and unity in the community. For example, the hunters together with farmers and cattle keepers come together to overcome a threat that would cause harm to their activities and families. The unity culture is also highlighted when it comes to the sharing of meat. They all understand the importance of sharing equally fruits of collective efforts. Also advised is the idea of faith and trust, where different women were being counseled not to underestimate their respective husbands when it comes to their particular responsibilities.

In the proverb *"Rumors ended up in Gishike"* the narrator emphasizes the magnitude of hatred, jealousy, and how very sensitive conspiracies are to the society hence they should not be given a space. This is manifested when people suspected and accused Rugereka over the death of King Mutara Rwogera. It was untrue and should not have caused disunity between Rwandese people and Abagereka. In the proverb *"He reaches Yihande horizons"* the narrator highlights different inappropriate behaviors which include conspiracies, brutality, disrespect and egoism; all these drove King Ruganzu Bwimba into a war which he could not have fought, and he lost his life and Rwanda lost their king. However, the speaker acknowledges the idea of maturity and fair judgment, where he describes the young King Cyirima Rugwe as royally immature yet manages to deliver a fair judgment after a discussion over a killed antelope while punishing those who failed to abide by the rules of war.

In the proverb *"Words attain Ndabaga's phase"* or *"Things attain Ndabaga's phase"* the speaker talks about patience and extreme commitment. Patience is portrayed in the character of Ndabaga's mother, the wife of Nyamutezi who had gone into a long-time battle camp. Ndabaga's love for her family and country generates commitment to go beyond her femininity and train herself in male tasks and she manages to get his father, the king, to regulate a new rule which would not keep older people at the battle camps.

In the proverb *"Not everything fine is entirely perfect"* the narrator strictly condemns the impunity of the two royal characters King Yuhi Mazimpaka and his son Cyirima Rujugira over Kalira's husband and brother. He again exposes how jealousy can result into unreasonable and atrocious killings, like what Mazimpaka did to his son

Musigwa. Additionally, in the proverb the narrator highly demonstrates the idea of self-sacrifice, determination, flexibility and integrity as manners that can help people to enhance communalism for a prosperous future in the country. This is shown in the proverb *"He is not a man, but a strong tree"* where the narrator stresses the gallantry of the legend Ruganzu Ndoli who revived the country after it vanished for 11 years, liberating and expanding it to far ends of the horizons.

In the proverb *"Keep your food, if you don't know the story at Fumbwe"* the idea of unreasonablly extended and occupational warfare is looked down upon, since it presents and bears no other importance other than imperialism and selfish domination. This is shown on how Bunyoro community fought Rwanda just to overtake it; they called on for an extra support from neighboring dynasties. However, the speaker values the importance of fighting a war under practical and plausible reasons which might be for the welfare of the community. This has been practically illustrated when the King Mibambwe Sekarongoro Mutabazi, instead of fighting with Bunyabungo community, who had initially offered them a refuge, over a dead bull decided to fight Bunyoro and get back the country to its people.

In the proverbs *"Measure your beehive to Bugegera's one"* the narrator once again speaks to us about the ideas of efficiency and a positive vision. Finally, in the last proverb *"The venue is at Huro"*, the narrator disssociates himself with longtime jealousies, choosing rather to stress the habit of common sociability and friendliness.

In conclusion the current study argues that historically, literary and culturally, proverbs have been influencing each other in as far as patriotism and heroism are concerned to the Rwandese community; and that deep in themselves, they are used not only to trace the history but also to suggest, adjust and/or change some behaviours within the community. It is in this regard that the study has sought to establish the relationship existing between these meta-genres and their historical trends while determining the role of Insigamigani texts as key guidance to the Rwandese daily life situation. We have limited the focus of this study to a collection of Benedigito Mulihano"s *"Ibirari By"insigamigani" (2005)* in collaboration with the Rwandese Ministry of Culture and Sport. The study has been a library based research and is a critical examination of how themes of heroism and patriotism are portrayed in Insigamigani documents.

Chapter 4

Rumuji Women's Dance

K I Clive

MOST African traditional societies before the contact with Western civilization practiced double decent which allowed kinship to be both patrilineal and matrilineal. Thus patriarchy was not rigid and rapacious. The rapacious nature of patriarchy became evident with the advent of western capitalism which disarticulated the socio-culture fabrics of traditional societies. Western patriarchy, redefined as capitalism, located creative labour in the hands of men while the creative labour and voice of women were subsumed in a male identity. This withdrawal of their identity and creative labour restricted women in the community. Thus creative labour and artistry grew to be regarded as works of heroic men and the gods in post-colonial analyses. Since the voice of women was mainly heard in the artistry of the male folks, women were regarded as incapable of creative and intellectual work.

Pre-colonial societies of Nigeria, particularly the Ikwerre from where this work locates, encouraged a wide variety of human expression. All the human components of the community had their expression in the community including the voice of women both in creative labour and artistry. The women shared the knowledge of plants, crafts herbs, crops, music and other indigenous activities. This dynamic nature of the indigenous community is expressed in creative performance where dance has a social significance because of its religious, symbolic and semiotic values. Dance tends to endow social acts with significance and meaning. The traditional dance is highly aesthetic and its beauty lies in its combination of purposiveness, its reflection of communal life, the embodiment of collective beliefs with its intensity of expression. Rumuji women dance as an ethnic forum for intra-inter group communication relocates the lost voice of women in society and creates a vibrant identity for the women, thus narrowing the social distance between the sexes in the community.

Women in Colonial/ Post-Colonial Period

The desire of people to be involved in the management of their affairs, the need to be active in areas where modern agencies are unwilling to act, and the development of new communication, relations that convey information and help people interact meaningfully; all these have encouraged women's voice in post colonial societies. Erstwhile the voice of women was sought in campaigns, boycotts, and conferences. Such schemes which became effective venue for women rights and human rights have been integrated into public thinking and inter-group negotiations. The clamour for more participation of women in modern cultural creation, distribution and consumption shows that more proactive processes have to be evolved which calls for the analysis of post colonial women's voice and their status. The colonial status and location of the voice of women was predicated on the restriction that the colonial government placed on women. The position of women and their voice changed in indigenous Nigerian societies when the colonial administration disrupted the traditional production machinery in favour of the men, thus reinforcing systems of social inequality. Parpart Jane affirms the opinion of most African scholars that the production forces of colonial government engendered unequal social relations in Africa and in Nigeria in particular. She notes:

For most African women, the colonial period was characterized by significant losses in both power and authority. Colonial offices accepted gender stereotypes which assigned women to domestic domain, leaving economic and political matters to men... colonial officials ignored potential female candidates for chief-ships, scholarship and other. (210)

The colonial period also lacked ethical frameworks in positions of social relations and production relationships which had concomitant effects in the disorganization of the erstwhile cohesive societies. This colonial prototype has been the carrier of development programmes and values in the evaluation of social relationships in post-colonial Nigeria. While the colonial legacy lacked a frame work for the transition of time tested values and relationships, it created a leap without recourse to the transformation of reward systems and forms of cultural creation. Colonial efforts suppressed effective cultural values as well as women's voice and implanted subterfuges. Rita Afsar in her research findings in Bangladesh asserts:

For the first time women constitute a significant proportion of the formal manufacturing labour force challenging their statistical "invisibility" and defying the patriarchal norms that constrain their visibility on the streets and in the factories. There were also positive indications from micro-level research that industrial wage work and women's enhanced contributions to their families are survival strategies providing the option for some women at least of renegotiating the terms of unsatisfactory relationships. (7)

The invisibility of women in the urban sector, a creation of post-colonial legacy, prompted the loss of women's productive and wage/ labour power. Due to the western stereotype of patriarchy which wrested power and authority from women, the work, voice and contribution of women are not measured appropriately. The docility and invisibility of women both in the process of cultural creation as well as the streets are pivoted on the unequal social relations provided by the forces of capitalist paid labour. This relationship which denied women voice and identity both in social, political and even religious rites has been accepted as the original, as well as ideal, measure of social relationships.

Thus the location of women in the unsatisfactory social relations based on the disrupted natural economy has further made women not only lose voice in the community due to the absence of legitimate authority but also butts of marital situations that undermine their dignity. The point being stressed here is that this subterfuge relationship has been accepted by the women who further deplete their willpower to address the dislocation in the process of power and social relationships. That there is the need for the reappraisal of institutions by taking into account social relations that make women invisible cannot be overstressed. This gender perspective means recognizing that women today stand at the crossroads between production and reproduction, between economic activity and the care of human beings, and therefore between economic growth and human development. Post-colonial women suffer the most and are always at crossroads in both public and domestic spheres. Women, like the men who control the economic, political and social activities of post-colonial societies, should have equal access to participate in the production processes so as to remove their invisibility and upgrade their dignity as well.

This work so far reflects upon the specific social forces through which women slide into invisibility and poverty. The central concern however focuses on the change in the institutional scope of women's participation and involvement in society. Inter-group and intra-group conflicts as well as social inequality are as old as man. However, what is strange and intriguing, particularly in the 21st century, is the heightened nature of inter-group dissension. The widening gap between the sexes in post-colonial situations has denied women access to decision-making processes which further stifles their voice both in the domestic circles and on the streets. An analysis of the situation reveals that the poor institutional transfer from pre-colonial to post-colonial structures aided the denial of women from participation in key processes of post-colonial community activities. The point is that the western worldview in the transfer of institutions deepened the invisibility of women in post-colonial societies.

Women's Voice in Pre-Colonial Communities

The processes of human participation in pre-colonial societies encouraged a wide range of human expression including the voice and participation of women. The age grade system and particularly, the women age grade dance groups were participatory forms of human governance that involved all categories of people in the community. Margaret Peil holds that in pristine traditional societies of Africa, there was bilateral decent: "a mixture of patriarchy and matriarchy" (4). She explains that while patriarchy held kin groups and lineages together, matriarchy was the driving force of identity and unity. Central in the work of Margaret Peil is the issue of kin group solidarity centered on the mother identity. Matriarchy and patriarchy did not induce polarity in the sexes but rather encouraged equity gender situations. In several situations in the Nigerian cultural milieu, and particularly in the Niger Delta, matriarchy and patriarchy are twin engines of cultural development. To isolate one in preference for the other is to endanger the community since both are all indices of cultural expression and identity.

The bond of matriarchy and patriarchy in pre-colonial societies is evident in burial situations where the deceased must be mourned and buried by the mother's people. Among the Ikwerre from where the work is based, the chief or the male must celebrate the mother's identity by going to live with the mother's people for weeks at a certain stage of life as a rite of passage. As Krama affirms:

It is also important to note that occupational roles determine characterization to some extent. Roles are not mutually exclusive to sex. Both men and women play roles that are not gender ascribed but functional to the realization of the communal spirit. Most of the cultural prescriptions on roles are not based on superiority but rather complementary. Depending on the challenges posed by the environment and social relationships particularly in matrilineal or patrilineal societies both sexes may play complementary roles. (51-52)

The Dance: Origin/Nomenclature

In pre-colonial communities, the age grade dance is a forum for the expression of the women and inter-group communication. The dance has the women as dancers, singers and drummers. Evident here is the artistry of the women performed by women and not as women performing male roles or parts. The artistry expressed in these dances is a reflection of communal ethos. Haberman has considered the relationship between social beings and social consciousness as the object and subject of history. He distinguishes between instrumental action and strategic action. The former he refers to as the action of a single actor who rationally calculates the best means to be adopted in pursing goals. The later involves two or more people who co-ordinate purposive rational action which aims at communication or understanding within the group.

Women's age grade dance, which is classified as folk dance, predates recorded history and is an integral part of the rites of passage which help to pressure their components of history. Enekwe has shown that the centre of the dynamic Nigerian dance is the indigenous community where dance has a social significance. Because of its religions, symbolic and semiotic values, the dance tends to endow social acts with legal significance and meaning (64). Enekwe emphasizes the axiological role of the age grade dance, particularly that of women, in constructing and sharing of both social as well as cultural imagery and maintains that the beauty of the age grade dance lies in its combination of purposiveness and high aesthetic concern which seeks to celebrate communal women's perception of life. The dance is an embodiment of collective beliefs and aspirations which constitute part of the cultural fabric of traditional society (64).

The traditional women's age grade dance is a key process of cultural creation and a connective nexus in traditional societies. Specifically the dance group reconstructs and constructs society through music and dance thus spurring communication as well as social action in the community. With the age grade dance women function as custodian of performing traditions, oral history and, therefore, kernels of veritable social and cultural functionaries in the sustenance and survival of traditional societies. The women's age grade dance functions not only for entertainment and group understanding of traditional norms but also as repertoires of indigenous knowledge and productive processes. These women also function both as mid-wives in traditional health care delivery and as counselors or moral incubators right from the home to the streets. Therefore women's voice is visible in the traditional community because the age grade dance locates actively in social, political and cultural activities of the community.

Rumuji Dance Performance

Rumuji community consists of five villages and the villages are between fourteen and fifteen compounds. Each compound has an age grade dance group which generates the name and identity of the dance group. The dance groups are of two kinds. The women married from outside the community have their own separate dance group known as the *Elerenyazi*. While the free born or those married within the village or community are known as *Rumurenya*. Both the *Elerenyazi* and the *Rumurenya* have the same composition as well as aim in creating identity for the women folk. The need also for equal representation and total participation of the women in communal activities as well as social activities necessitated the formation of the groups from the compounds. Membership to the compound women age grade dance is automatic once married to the compound or born in the compound. The different age grade women's dance groups have in common Women in Council (WIC) and Women Community Development Committee (WCDC). Both exist in every village that makes up the Rumuji community. The Women Community Development Committee ensures development based projects that are of direct benefit to the people. They function as a community based organization that liaises with both internal and outside agencies. The Women in Council (WIC) are elderly members of the group who bring women's issues to the council of rulers in the community. These members are highly respected and share the same status with *Ofo* title holders. In an oral interview, Chief (Mrs.) Nyeche notes that "this particular group of women does not talk anyhow and they are well respected in the community. They even go bare footed like the *Ofo* holders because they are seen as people close to the gods". The Women in Council ensure that problems do not persist in the community. These women settle both intra and inter group problems. These women have a nick name, *Ikeare/renwu* (bees). They are called bees because people avoid them in the case of a problem. In a related interview, Chisa Abel explains thus:

The women age grade dancing group is the voice of women that celebrate their womanhood, artistry and beauty. Therefore the chant, Elenya-ma, Oyoyo used by the women during meetings and dance calls the women to their responsibilities in the community. (Np)

The women performances which as social performances are opposed to the various sacred rites performed by the men in the community. The meetings which involve music and dance centre on welfare of women primarily. Therefore such issues as burials, widows, land tenure and general communal issues are also addressed.

The meetings and performance of the women age grade dance are regular and usually hold on the various compounds as well as play grounds. Most often members perform during burials both of members and family members. During performance the women usually dress in uniforms of either *George* wrapper or use a special local fabric. Only the women in council dress differently, they may tie only the wrapper above the waist and leave the breast bare because of their age. They also come with their local chairs from their homes. The group which is an all-women dance group has the women as dancers, singers, and drummers. The old women exhibit the traditional *acapella* and traditional dance steps for the young ones to learn from. At the community level, the women sit according to their villages or compounds and perform accordingly. Apart from discussing community issues women also have a local banking scheme where they contribute as savings during the meetings. These savings are shared at the end of the year. While some use the money for the next farming season others use theirs for social activities. One of the songs include:

1. Ainametele Rumuji,
Mebele owe (2x)
Chorus:
Aimelele Rumuji
Mehele owe (2x)

2. Mayameleko nu mini
wee ee (2x)
Chorus:
Nesowovaowovu,
Nwomeleko me mini
Wee, eee (2x)
Nesowovaoworu

In conclusion if we are to locate the cause of women's invisibility in urban society we must trace the inequitable transfer of institutions which affected the appropriation of women's artistry and voice during the colonial and post-colonial periods. Our look at the pre-colonial traditional society however indicates that participation and representation of women was active in the traditional community and that patriarchy in the pre-colonial societies was not as rapacious as in post-colonial societies especially in the urban situation.

The recommendation implicit in this study is that existing institutional frameworks should be reassessed to strengthen those institutions that were jettisoned during the establishment of post-colonial structures. Moreover proactive agencies should rediscover the lost values that maintain a balance in the transformation of ideas, people and their institutions. The women's age grade and dance groups of pre-colonial societies as evident among Rumuji women could be reassessed and redirected into modern development processes to encourage wider participation of rural dwellers in cultural creation. Finally this work locates the relevance of traditional values in the continuation and development of African societies in order to curb the present political/ social invisibility of women in society.

Chapter 5

Time and the Traditional Palimpsest

K Okajima

IN his influential work, *How Europe Underdeveloped Africa*, Walter Rodney critically examines the impact of the slave trade in Africa showing how the European slave trade systematically underdeveloped the African continent. However, despite the tremendous influence that the slave trade exerted on every corner of contemporary African life, most West African writers appeared to turn away from the traumatic memory of the slave trade, pursuing milder themes of pre-colonial Africa or post-colonial challenges of emerging nations. Indeed critics and scholars have read Ben Okri's 1991 novel *The Famished Road* as such a novel.

For instance, Olatubosun Ogunsarwo, focusing on the narrative modes of the novel, celebrates the magical-realist framework used to create the typical "postcolonial" novel (50). Ogunsarwo argues that the juxtaposition of the African folkloric myth with the description of the nation's predicament in form of a European realist novel signals the discursive multiculturality of "postcolonial" conditions, which allegedly re-formulates the colonial perception of different cultural phenomena. Ogunsarwo maintains "The inescapable intertextuality and the consequent mutual 'rubbing off' underline the interdiscursivity of the novel's textual discourse; there is a relation of mutual interdependence between the dominated and the dominators that must be recognized, since neither the imperial city nor the colony can return to a 'pure' state following colonization" (45). Along similar lines, John C. Hawley applies the label "postcolonial postmodernity" to *The Famished Road*, asserting that "The significance of an *abiku* narrator … is that it moves African literature closer to the postmodern movement" (31 his italics). According to Hawley, Azaro's presence as an abiku child embodies alternative ontological systems that are foreign to the western master narrative of history while at the same time Azaro allegorizes postmodern "resistance to the fixing of boundaries" that enable him to "imagine something new" (36). On balance, these scholars praise the happy blending of essential elements of the African mythological consciousness with the postmodern stylistic features, which ultimately creates this "postcolonial" novel.1 While such arguments may have its own credits, their rather easy celebration of the "postcolonial" hybridity seems to overlook the significance of the traumatic memory of the colonialism that is still alive and manifest in Okri's novel.

On closer reading, *The Famished Road* could bear some memories of the transatlantic slave trade. Following M. Jacqui Alexander's palimpsestic notion of time, we can trace Azaro's repetitive movements between the worlds of the Living and the Unborn as symbolic of the slave trade. African sentiments on the slave trade may also be illustrated in Azaro's parents' reaction toward their son's unstable movements between the two worlds. Thus, Ben Okri's novel could serve to save the memory of the colonial violence that was inflicted on Africa from oblivion through Azaro's palimpsestic existence that perpetually re-scrambles the past and present.

2. The "Black Hole" in African History and Literature

Laura Murphy points out an apparent consensus among African scholars that Africa lacks collective memory of the Atlantic slavery (Murphy 141). As quoted by Murphy in her essay "Into the Bush of Ghosts: Specters of the Slave Trade in West African Fiction," Bogumil Jewsiewichi and V.Y. Mudimbe argue that African intellectuals "establish a direct link between a glorious past and a future, while bypassing the barbarism of foreign intrusion" (9).2 Jewsiewichi and Mudimbe further claim "The result is a black hole, a huge omission, which, by the very structure of suspended time, is excluded from history" (10). In other words, African scholars ignore the traumatic periods of the colonial history in favor of the pre-colonial history that incarnates the traditional, mythical Africa or simply the usable past. At stake here is the selectiveness with which African intellectuals reconstruct African history.

It is significant then that contemporary West African literature also appears to reflect this whimsical conception of history. Kwadwo Opoku-Agyemang states:

"The vastest depth and stretches of African history, slavery and the slave trade are never regarded in a sustained way or mined in any serious fashion for their lessons, their truths and their metaphors. ... [and that] Modern African literature, then, is essentially a literature of forgetfulness, and the evidence is related to a gap in our history four hundred years long" (quoted in Murphy 142). This echoes Murphy's comment that West African writers turn away from the traumatic history of the slave trade, focusing instead on present-day concerns such as poverty and government corruption (142).

The Famished Road has been read as a part of the "literature of forgetfulness" as it apparently focuses on the struggles that contemporary Nigerian people face. Unique to *The Famished Road* is how the struggle for the birth of the nation is modeled after the Nigerian mythological tradition, namely, the myth of the abiku spirit-child. Abiku, literally "born to die," is a spirit who does not wish to be born and resists life by willing itself to die in infancy. Azaro, the narrator protagonist, is one of such abiku children. Azaro delineates the characteristics of abiku children who reside in the "world of the Unborn":

As we approached another incarnation we made pacts that we would return to the spirit world at the first opportunity. We made these vows in fields of intense flowers and in the sweet-tasting moonlight of that world. Those of us who made such vows were known among the Living as abiku, spirit-children. ... We were the ones who kept coming and going, unwilling to come to terms with life. We had the ability to will our deaths. Our pacts were binding. (Okri 4)

Azaro, however, does not follow this destiny. He abandons his companions, choosing instead to stay with his parents in the world of the Living. The main plot of the novel, if any, is that Azaro's spirit companions come to take him back to the spirit world, causing much trouble for Azaro and his parents though Azaro consistently resists and escapes them.

It is noteworthy that Azaro's struggle for birth corresponds with Nigeria's struggle for independence. In other words, set in 1960s urban Nigeria, Okri's novel depicts Nigeria's slow, painful emergence from British colonialism. This interesting similarity between the abiku child and the nation is clearly shown in the text. Toward the end of the novel, Azaro narrates his father's thoughts on their nation whose destiny, according to his father, is comparable to that of abiku child, "Dad found that all nations are children; it shocked him that ours too was an abiku nation, a spirit-child nation, one that keeps being reborn and after each birth come blood and betrayals, and the child of our will refuses to stay till we have made propitious sacrifice and displayed our serious intent to bear the weight of a unique destiny"(494). The crucial implication here is that *The Famished Road* can be read as part of the "literature of forgetfulness" in the sense that the novel combines traditional Nigerian myth with contemporary issues of independence, apparently leaving out the painful memory of the slave trade.

3. Palimpsestic Time as *Anti* Post-colonialism

The concept of post-coloniality has required us that we rationalize the numerous colonizing operations still taking place today. Concerning this point, Carole Boyce-Davies contends that we are not beyond Western colonialism and the ideologies of "posting" work to re-hegemonize Western cultures: "Post-coloniality represents a misnaming of current realities, it is too premature a formulation, it is too totalizing, it erroneously contains decolonizing discourse" (61). Boyce-Davies further argues "(T)he effect has been a highly problematic subsuming of non-Western cultures, reducing these cultures while further hegemonizing the West" (61). Boyce-Davies emphasizes that the postness of post-colonialism is a false claim; in effect, colonialism has a lingering effect and still torments the colonized.

In the light of Boyce-Davies' understanding of post-coloniality, we can read *The Famished Road* differently. It is plausible to argue Azaro/Nigeria's prolonged struggle for birth describes their battle with lingering colonialism. In fact, neither Azaro nor Nigeria secures life in the novel. Their circumstances are open-ended. The novel is directionless, emphasizing the repetitive events: Azaro's capture and escape from his spirit-companions. Hence, it is of great import to note that *The Famished Road* defies the ideology of "posting." In this sense, it is *anti* post-colonialism. Implicit within the discourse of post-colonialism is a notion of time that is linear and hierarchical. Contrary to the linear flow of time, Okri's novel offers an alternative sense of time, namely palimpsestic conception of time that defies the ideology of "posting."3

In *Pedagogies of Crossings: Meditations on Feminism, Sexual Politics, Memory, and the Sacred*, M. Jacqui Alexander conceptualizes this notion, proposing a deconstruction of the Western linear flow of time. Alexander states,

> Time is neither vertically accumulated nor horizontally teleological. ... The central idea is that of the palimpsest -- a parchment that has been imperfectly erased and remaining therefore still partly visible. ... It thus rescrambles the "here and now" and the "then and there" to a 'here and there' and a 'then and now,' and makes visible ... the ideological traffic between and among formations that are positioned as dissimilar. (190)

It is noteworthy that the palimpsestic concept of time dovetails with Azaro's circumstance as an abiku child who experiences life and death repetitively:

> I was still very young when in a daze I saw Dad swallowed up by a hole in the road. Another time I saw Mum dangling from the branches of a blue tree. I was seven years old when I dreamt that my hands were covered with the yellow blood of a stranger. I had no idea whether these images belonged to this life, or to a previous one, or to one that was yet to come, or even if they were merely the host of images that invades the minds of all children. When I was very young I had a clear memory of my life stretching to other lives. There

were no distinctions. Sometimes I seemed to be living several lives at once. One lifetime flowed into the others and all of them flowed into my childhood. (Okri 7)

It is important that Azaro's confusion works to disrupt the linear flow of time and thus has potential to fill in the "black hole" in African history. In other words, Azaro's different perception of time enables the memory of the slave trade to come to surface of the text. Indeed, the image is a recurring motif in Azaro's life that is based on the scrambled "then and now" formulation of time.

4. Images of Slave Trade and the African Sentiment

Azaro's struggles with his spirit-companions who come to take him back to their world are comparable to the vicious cycles of the slave trade.4 In a significant scene depicting the image of the slave trade, spirit-companions kidnap Azaro in a sack at Madam Koto's bar.5 In this scene, albinos, Azaro's spirit-companions disguised as humans, come to capture him:

And then the albinos sprang at me and covered me with the sack. I struggled and fought, but they expertly bundled me in and tied up the sack as if I were an animal. And as I resisted, kicking, I heard the noises of the world, the voices of all the different people who had been in the bar. ....They took me down many roads, rough-handling me in the sack. ....All the time I fought and struggled like a trapped animal. The more I strained for freedom, the more they tightened the sack, till I had no room to struggle. (Okri 111-112)

Here Azaro's kidnap in a bag, shrouded by darkness and unable to move, signals the state of being buried alive. This resonates with Harriet Jacobs's account of her captivity in the attic of her grandmother's house where the boundary between life and death is destabilized in a complete darkness. As Jacobs suggests, the dark attic is comparable to a tomb where she is buried alive. Jacobs' account of the ambiguous borderline between life and death succinctly explicates the predicament of captured slaves who lack freedom and are totally subordinated. In this sense, it seems plausible to read Azaro's being abiku-child who is, in a way, both alive and dead as a metaphor for slavery. All in all, Azaro's captivity in a sack is a re-imagined description of the traumatic experiences of Africans.

Another significant motif that denotes mnemonic traces of the slave trade is found in the trope of eating, or what Saidiya Hartman calls "the politics of belly" (114). The trope of eating provides a clear picture of the relationship between the powerful and the powerless or the captor and the enslaved. In other words, in a metaphorical sense, the slaves are devoured by their captors and masters as food. As Hartman asserts "Who could deny that white men gained their strength from black flesh? It was clear for everyone to see: they possessed the power to transform the bones of slaves into gunpowder, to convert blood into wine, and to dine on their organs" (69). Interestingly, Okri's novel is replete with the trope of being eaten. The politics of belly is unequivocally linked with the slave trade in peculiar images of roads that eat people. Azaro's parents frequently caution him about the roads. One time, Azaro's Mum says "The roads swallow people and sometimes at night you can hear them calling for help, begging to be freed from the inside its stomach" (Okri 121). Mum's caution resonates with Dad's oral tradition about the King of the Road. According to Dad, the King of the Road is a legendary giant who eats travelers on the road:

Once upon a time ... there was a giant whom they called the King of the Road. ... The King of the Road had a huge stomach and nothing he ate satisfied him. So he was always hungry. Anyone who wanted to travel on the road had to leave him a sacrifice or he would not allow them to pass. Sometimes he would even eat them up. ... Anyone who forgot the monster's existence sooner or later got eaten up. ... Some say people make sacrifices to the road to remember that the monster is still there and that he can rise at any time and start to eat up human beings again. ... That is why a small boy like you must be very careful how you wander about in this world (258-261).

The oral tradition about the King of the Road may be read as a slave narrative in the contemporary African imagination. It is noteworthy that the story about the hungry King of the Road is directly linked with the title of the novel, *The Famished Road*. In a metaphorical sense, the roads ruled by the King of the Road can be compared to the slave trails leading to the Atlantic Ocean. Historically, the slave trails were a space where African lives began to end. In other words, it embodied a door of no return. To borrow Hartman's words, the slave trail "is a road of torment and devastation, a road of insatiable and cruel appetites, a road where you lost everything" (181). Indeed, in the novel, each time Azaro is captured by spirits, he is taken along the roads that lead to water that symbolizes the Atlantic. Azaro's travels metaphorically denote the routes taken by slaves. That is why both Mum and Dad warn Azaro of the roads.

Even in the history of the transatlantic slave trade, "cannibal" roads not only functioned as a metaphor, but also existed in reality. During the era of the slave trade, castles were built along the coast lines as a storehouse of the enslaved. Cape Coast Castle in Ghana is one such castle built by the British. This castle in fact functioned as the cannibal King that devoured the slaves. As Hartman's travel narrative from Ghana explicates, the dungeon in the castle resembled a large intestine. Moreover, in 1972, a team of archaeologists excavated the dungeon and found out that the top layer of the floor consisted of the compressed remains of captives such as feces, blood, and skin (Hartman 115). Indeed, the castle devoured the enslaved. It is no coincidence that Azaro's parents talk about the cannibalistic roads. The apparently mythic story about the King of the Road in fact has existential reality.

As to the ways in which African sentiments on slavery are expressed in the text, we find Azaro, after being heavily scolded by his parents, refusing to eat and, as a form of revenge, slowly departing from the world of the Living, while his crying parents cling hopefully on him:

On the third day of refusing to eat, I began to leave the world. Everything became distant. I willed myself away, wanting to leave, singing the songs of departures that only my spirit companions can render with the peculiar beauty of flutes over desolate mountains. Mum's face was far away. The distance between us grew. Dad's face, large and severe, no longer frightened me. His assumption that the severity of his features gave him power over anything made him look a little comical. I punished him by retreating from the world. I tortured them both by listening with fullness of heart to the unsung melodies of spirit companions. ...I did not sleep for three days. I did not eat. Mum wept. She seemed a long way off, in a remote part of the earth. I ranged deeper into that world. (Okri 325)

Azaro starts travelling with the three-headed spirit on the road that leads to the river separating the two worlds. While Azaro journeys to the spirit world, he is still connected to the world of the Living, able to see and hear what his parents do or say to him. Indeed, it is Azaro's parents who stops him from leaving and takes him back to their world. Dad says to Azaro:

We are poor. *We have little to give you, but our love.* You came out of our deepest joy. We prayed for you. We wanted you. ...Don't you feel for us? Every moment that my head is bursting with loads at the garage, my soul is brimming with good dreams for you. In this life you have seen how sweet even sorrow can be. Our life appears to be a sad music. So how can you come and then leave us? Do you know our misery? Do you know how you make even that bearable? (337italics added)

Saying that they love Azaro, Dad attempts to persuade him not to go. This sentiment, "because we love you, don't go," is what Africans felt for the enslaved who left for another world. It is noteworthy that this sentiment is reflected in the term *odonkor*. *Odonkor* is an Akan word that refers to someone bought and sold at market. That is, *odonkor* means slave. Nonetheless, its etymology paradoxically embraces the African sentiment toward the slaves. The origins of the word are in the words *odo* - "love"- and *nti nka*, meaning "don't go" (Hartman 87). Therefore, *Odo nti nka* means "Because of our love, don't go." Eventually, Azaro's parents successfully take him back to their world by expressing their love to him. It is his parents' love that saves Azaro.

The Famished Road describes the mnemonic traces of the slave trade through Azaro's palimpsestic existence, refusing the linear, hierarchical ideologies of "posting." As we have seen, the novel also accurately captures the African sentiment toward the enslaved: the eternal bonding to the beloved, and to roots. In this sense, it seems entirely possible to read this novel as Okri's attempt to fill the "black hole" in African history. To put it differently, *The Famished Road* is the novel that aims to save the memory of the prolonged colonial violence meted out to the continent from oblivion. Okri resurrects the remembrance of the buried past in the way that Azaro's parents saved their son through the expression of love.

Chapter 6

Poetics of African Naming

G N Shang

THE issue of language has been a central question in Ngugi's texts, essays, lectures, and civic activism. Ngugi's engagement with language is based on a Fanonian premise that the use of the imperial language entails a symbolic appropriation of its world view, a process that alienates the writer and the (post)colonial subject from his socio-cultural milieu: "To speak means to be in a position to use a certain syntax, to grasp the morphology of this or that language, but it means above all to assume a culture, to support the weight of civilization" (Fanon 17). As a writer who seeks to represent the consciousness of the oppressed peripheral voices in the postcolonial polity, Ngugi has, especially in *Decolonising the Mind*, forcefully and consistently argued in favour of the use of African language by the African writer as a necessary means of negotiating his Africanity and his unity with his people.

Although he follows up his ideology by writing most of his works after *Petals of Blood* in Kikuyu, Ngugi never eschewed English language as a medium of literary expression. His Kikuyu written works have ultimately been followed by their English versions. The present text, *Wizard of the Crow* was first written in Kikuyu before being translated by the author himself into English. Unlike some francophone African writers (for example Sony Labou Tansi and Ahmadou Kourouma) who have sought to disfigure the colonial language and 're-occupy' its epistemic system, Ngugi's expression in *Wizard of the Crow* is not defined by any such intention to inflect the English language. Our focus on his language therefore addresses his representation of the power to name, to order and to ordain character/events and how such a system contributes to the author's conception of the subject and the community.

For Ngugi therefore naming constitutes an important aspect of his representation of language, power and worldview. A major trait of Ngugi's *Wizard of the Crow* is the capacity to condition existence through naming and to provide the frame through which events, persons and processes are perceived. A name does not only address what is named, it redresses, restitutes it and re-defines its relationship with other entities in the world. We would therefore base this essay on the proclivity of the text to dispute, contest and reconstitute names in the negotiation of power relations within the postcolonial society. From this perspective, a name is not only a noun, it is a metaphor, a conceit, an allegory and a narrative that determines the course/cause of the character/event along the plotline of the text. To 're-name' is therefore to review, to revisit the trajectory, to re-plot the narrative and to re-cast what is renamed in a new image. In Ngugi's artistic frame, the name sets man into motion and through this, a new subject is born in the fulfillment of a destiny that is not only personal but equally and more importantly communal. We approach the question of 'naming' in *Wizard of the Crow* as an important factor in the understanding of subjectivity, collective consciousness, textual tonality and artistic vision.

In order to understand the system of naming in Ngugi's text, it is important to examine the author's self re-naming. It is not a rare practice for African authors to repudiate their Western-Christian names. However, it is the significance behind the re-naming that calls for critical analysis. In *Wizard of the Crow*, when Kamiti pretends to cure Tajirika of the speech malady of "ifs" and to exorcise him of his desire of to become a White man, he warns the latter: "A slave first loses his name, then his language. So Mr. Clarence Whitehead, you now know what to do next. Your language. Give it up." (182). This parody captures Ngugi's symbolic association of the question of language and naming to the bigger issue of identity and cultural imperialism. Eschewing the colonial name and re-naming the self is a symbolic exoneration of the colonial consciousness and cultural emaciation that the name evokes. In a cultural system where naming carries immense cultural signification and where the name putatively reflects its reference, naming constitutes an important aspect of the re-negotiation of self-identity and community construction in Ngugi's literary imagination. 'James Ngugi' rejected the Christian name 'James' which he considered as a mark of English colonialism and its Greco-Roman cultural corollary; a symbolic renunciation of colonial mentality. The renaming is therefore meant to position the author as the cultural voice of his community against (neo) colonialism. Self-renaming therefore represents a symbolic re-unification of the author with his community and its cultural memory. Through the poetics and politics of naming, Ngugi seeks to articulate the subject's condition of subjugation under neo-colonialism, cultural imperialism and capitalism. Even though Ngugi has consistently criticized Christianity, it is rather impossible to analyze his works without an in-depth grasp of the Biblical names and parables (Nazareth 13). His works are draped in Biblical metaphors, parables and allusions (and illusions). Moreover, biblical knowledge is necessary in the understanding of his vision of salvation, redemption and social regeneration.

Naming and Collective Consciousness

The process of individual and group consciousness is impossible to analyse without an adequate understanding of the system of naming of characters. The eponymous *Wizard of the Crow* is called "Kamiti," a name that seems benign to its bearer at the beginning but which gradually becomes the basis on which his relationship with the self and the outside world is negotiated. As the text unfolds, the pregnant nature of the name 'Kamiti' and its symbolic complexity take shape as the character undergoes various levels of transformations. "Kamiti" changes his identity in various episodes in the novel ranging from mistaken identity to quackery and simulacra. When the Wizard of the Crow[1] travels to New York as the State witch-doctor to 'heal' the Ruler from the strange illness of 'self-induced expansion', he is identified as "Abdi Manga" for security reasons (503). This is an attempt by the Ruler's government to conceal the fact that they are making recourse to magical powers to salvage the health of the ailing president. By re-naming Kamiti, they attempt to symbolically possess him so that his simulated magical powers can advance the course of the dictatorial regime. However, Kamiti uses his closeness with the centre of power to subvert the system and foster the agenda of the Movement for the voice of the people which organizes protests against the regime.

As a character whose identity vacillates according to the context in which he finds himself, Kamiti is the lifeline of the tortuous plot of Ngugi's novel. When he returns from India with an MBA, Kamiti roams the streets of Eldares hopelessly searching for a job. Dejected and guilty of his incapacity to honour his family that has sacrificed so much for his education, he gives in to alcoholism as a form of escapism and psychological relief:

Now he turned his pockets inside out and found enough to take to the counter. May be if he tossed down two or three beers he would feel good, he would at least forget the turn his life had taken. (68)

Tipsy from alcohol and wrecked by disillusion and shame, he decides to throw himself onto the garbage heap. However, when the garbage collectors come to clear the filth, Kamiti incidentally regains full consciousness and suddenly 'arises from death,' to the shock of the former who flee in shock and awe. The garbage collectors spread the news that they have met the 'devil' on the garbage heap. This leads to the 'spiritual warfare' against the devil by the 'Soldiers of Christ' of Santalucia. On the level of the main plot, Kamiti's 're-awakening marks the beginning of his determined efforts to survive which would later lead him into the practice of quackery/divination, enabling him to ignite power struggles between ministers who visit his shrine for better political appointments. Ngugi's parody of Judeo-Christian myth of re-birth is therefore central in the story of *Wizard of the Crow*. This incident is pregnant with dramatic irony. Even though the garbage collectors and the Soldiers of Christ consider Kamit as the devil's incarnate leading to their illusory and ludicrous crusade against his spirit, Kamiti represents the opposite in the narrative texture of Ngugi's text. In Christlike imagery, Kamiti represents the spirit of survival and regeneration amidst a dehumanizing system. Kamiti represents the regenerated spirit of an oppressed people, a fact he would only learn later in the novel.

With the woe brought to his family by politics, Kamiti's consciousness dithers on a sense of helplessness, victimhood and disillusion. Same as Wanja in Ngugi's *Petals of Blood* who comes to the Machiavellian conclusion that in post-independence

Kenya, "you either eat or you are eaten" (*72*), Kamiti comes to the verge of losing faith in social morality. However, if Wanja can use his womanhood as a means of survival, Kamiti has nothing on which to fall back. His transformation is therefore typical of Ngugi's archetypal heroes, who border on the precipice of resignation, defeatism and nihilism, just to come back more convicted and determined to fight for social justice. In Karega's[2] case, we are told: "He came very close to the fatal mistake of losing faith in the people and in the possibilities of truth and beauty and ideals in a world where people were daily struggling for bread and water: But he heard the voice of Wanja and Abdullah calling from a sudden plunge in the slough…" (253). While Karega's full consciousness and comprehension of the history of (neo) colonial oppression takes root during the odyssey to Ilmorog when he meets the lawyer, Kamiti makes an inverse trajectory to his native village. In *Wizard of the Crow*, Ngugi's Kamiti undergoes a similar transformation of consciousness. Prior to this journey and his meeting with Nyawira, Kamiti is apolitical, a result of bitter family memories:

His aversion to political engagement, especially mass movements, was shaped by the experiences of his family. His father, once a primary school teacher, had lost his job because of his attempt to unionize teachers in his area. And his grandfather had died in the war of independence. Political struggles had brought his family only misery, and he wanted nothing to do with them. Was it not ironic, then, that the very politics he had so pointedly tried to avoid were now being forced on him by the actions of others? (129)

In the background of disillusionment, Kamiti is later going to discover the seed of hope and the fountain of energy necessary for the continuation of the communal struggle. His journey to the village constitutes a moment of introspection, a voyage into the self, the family, clan and the society that would grant him insight into the history of slavery, colonialism, neo-colonialism (294). Moreover, what appears to him as a history of failure would be re-plotted along the lines of inspiration and hope. When he confides to his parents the news of his practice of divination, he is troubled by the fear that they would repudiate him in their expectation of a befitting and income-generating job. Contrariwise, his father perceives in his twist of fate the fulfillment of a prophecy. He narrates the life of his grandfather, Kamiti wa Kienjeku, his role in the liberation struggle, his gift of healing and his dedication to the service of his community.

The fact that Kamiti is born 'holding a shell' (295) foretells his divine 'election.' It confides on the child a spiritual mission: to re-unite the present with the ancestral spirit and culture of struggle, a major motif in the literary culture of Ngugi wa Thiong'o. The name Ka-Miti (294-5) means "child of the Miti clan", a community that was wrecked apart in the colonial days by the British conquest. Kamiti's journey to the village ends in the parental blessing for his practice of herbal treatment and his transformation from a state of parochial individualism to the level of spiritual consciousness and *Weltanschauung* of his community. From this perspective, *Wizard of the Crow* can be considered as *Bildungsroman* since it is developed along a narrative of progressive self-awareness and individual and group consciousness.

Through a reading of Kenya's independence struggle, it can be postulated that 'Kamiti' reflects the transfigured anagram of Dedan Kimathi, the charismatic head of the Kenya Land and Freedom Army popularly known as "Mau Mau" that fought against British colonialism. The image of Kimathi is an underlining myth that knits the variety of Ngugi's fictional and theatrical productions. Ngugi mythologizes the freedom fighter and inscribes him in an expanded temporality within the aesthetics of transcendence and Phoenix-like re-generation. In another dimension, the name 'Kamiti' also re-echoes the (in)famous prison house in Kenya where most of the Kenyan politicians were imprisoned under the heinous regime of Arap Moi.

The symbolic death and eventual resurrection of Kamiti could reflect a history of resilience, re-birth and renewal of the nation, which the Movement of the Voice of the People commemorates towards the end of the text. Thus, Ngugi's naming system represents a quest for unity, resistance and defiance against forces of exploitation and oppression. With the re-membering of the death of the nationalist fighters and the struggles of the new generations, Ngugi establishes a culture of resistance that continuously resurfaces and transcends various historical temporalities.

It is impossible to analyze the character of Kamiti without that of Nyawira. If his father educates him on the spiritual and metaphysical dimension of his character, it is the female figure of Nyawira that participates in broadening Kamiti's 'social' consciousness. Before meeting her "he was unaccustomed to making connections between his woes and those of the community at large" (6). This point is important because if Kamiti represents the history of resistance, Nyawira, the female Janus-face of Wizard of the Crow,[3] epitomizes social consciousness across various classes and communities. This gives a symbolic value to their friendship and the innuendo of their marriage towards the end of the text. In the same way as Ast and Asar in Armah's *Osiris Rising*, the sexual act that they intermittently perform constitutes a ritual of unity in the fight against oppression. It fuses the two characters into the equivocal voice/face of the Wizard of the Crow. When AG re-visits the shrine of the Wizard during Kamiti's trip to the village, he is addressed by a female voice. He leaves the shrine bewildered by the fact that the Wizard of the Crow can transform itself into male and female characters (274). The *con-fusion* of Kamiti and Nyawira (who is later on referred to as the Limping Witch when she penetrates the presidential palace to free Kamiti who has been arrested by presidential guards) represents the multifaceted nature of Ngugi's characters and the *theatricality* of Ngugi's prose. The spectacles of simulacra around characters, sustaining the anxiety of the reader through suspense, relating the main plot to finicky subplots in this gigantic text and finally unclothing the multiple folds of personality masks constitute major aspects of Ngugi's dexterity in storytelling.

Kamiti and Nyawira are the two sides of the same coin and the plot of the texts is advanced by their mutual complicity against the power elite. Though Nyawira's full name is Grace Nyawira, she tells Kamiti that "I prefer Nyawira by itself." (63). 'Grace' is considered as a remnant of colonialism and only her father calls her by that name. Unlike Karega in *Petals of Blood*, Nyawira lacks the proletarian background of Ngugi's typical Marxist characters for she hails from a relatively well-to-do family that had collaborated with the colonialists prior to independence. Her mercantilist father wishes to betroth her to an aristocrat, but Nyawira is independent-minded and refuses to be lured by a life of comfort and complacency. When she gets married to the artist Kanuiru, her father is disappointed and thereby disavows her. She decides unregrettably to live with Kanuiru in a union of hard work and dedication. However, she misjudges Kanuiru whose intention is to use her as a pawn to access her father's immense wealth. When she discovers Kanuiru's cloven hoof, she divorces him, dedicating her life to the struggle for democratic freedom in Aburiria. Detached from her family, she anchors herself in the collective struggles of her society: "Involvement in other people's suffering turned out to be the best way of coping with her personal woes, for she was able to see that these woes were not peculiar to her situation but were shared by many others" (428). Nyawira therefore posits as the moral voice in the text and the counterpoise of the boss of the Marching to

Heaven Project, Tajirika (who becomes president at the end of the narrative). The latter, whose name literally means "he who becomes rich", represents the ruling class, its intrigues, subterfuges, corruption and neo-colonial inclinations.

Ngugi's system of naming seeks to construct from multiple subjectivities and subjectifications, a communal "we" that participates in a history of struggle against neo-colonialism and dictatorship. However, Ngugi's 'we' is not based on the atomic fixation of identity and anchorage in a specific temporality. On the contrary, it posits itself as a cosmopolitan and not a parochial 'we', one that is based more on civic than ethnic identity. This could account for the shift of the text's setting from the Kamiti clan to 'Eldares' the capital of Aburiria, 'Eldares,' where most of the episodes in the text take place could represent a literary transfiguration of the cosmopolitan Kenyan town of 'Eldoret.' As such, Ngugi's 'we' is also a civic and culturally complex one whose diversity is 'mobilized' for a united struggle against oppression. It symbolizes the transformation of a folk, nationalist *gemeinschaft* (community) into the civic and patriotic *gesellschaft* (society) that is under construction.

Through the cosmopolitan nature of 'Eldares,' the text adopts affiliative as opposed to filiative approach to collective consciousness. According to Edward Said, filiation stresses a common genealogy while affiliation is based on civic interests and the desire to construct a more representative polity (19-20). It is through affiliation that the Movement for the Voice of the People subverts and deconstructs the parochial governing clique with their restricted cronyism and limited notion of citizenship.

The members of the ruling class are named following a system of nomenclature that exposes the decadent practices of postcolonial power. It is from this perspective that we talk about the Rabelaisian influence on the system of naming in Ngugi wa Thiong'o's text with its use of humour, magical realism and baroque hyperbolisations. The key ministers of the Ruler's regime indulge in plastic surgery to prove their loyalty to the Ruler. Markus Yawe Macho Kali, the minister of foreign affairs increases his eyeballs "so that he can be able to spot the enemies of the Ruler no matter how far in their hiding places [...] enlarged to the size of electric bulbs, his eyes were now the most prominent feature of his face, dwarfing his nose, cheeks, and forehead...And so Machokali he became, and later on forgot the name given at his birth" (*Wizard* 13).

The new name sets into being a new person, acting out the rules of his self-attributed identity. The habit of plastic surgery is copied by Sikiokku (Minister in charge of State Security) and Big Ben Jumbo (Minister in charge of (mis)information) who enlarge their ears and tongue respectively to rival Machokali in 'serving' the Ruler. However, the character Machokali is the most pertinent in Ngugi's parody on (re)naming. In as much as Machokali enters the fiction of his new personality, he also serves as the 'spin doctor' of the regime in creating realities through his oratorical skills.

In the world of the Republic of Aburiria, public performances and rituals come into concrete reality through the system of naming. When the women, through their dance, expose their butts to the presidential tribune as a ritual of desecration and defiance during the visit of the Global Bank delegates, Machokali still finds the appropriate words and the discursive power to transform the scatological performance into a gesture of endorsement and ratification of the Ruler's regime:

He tried to be glib, reminding the people that they were after all in black Africa, and what they had seen and heard was black humour from an ancient Aburirian ritual. But before elaborating on the ritual and its significance, he glanced at all his guests to see how they were taking his attempt at humour only to see them all staring at something. (252)

What the women enact through their bodies, the state attempts to transform and re-signify through the discursive power of the word. It is when, through the surrealist mood, the guests see the stage crumbling that they can factor the reality of the subversive gesture. In the same way, Machokali and his colleagues in the government use various discourses to define the queue mania depending on the interests of the Ruler. Though the power of re-naming succeeds temporarily, the corrupt government does not succeed in obtaining funding for the white elephant project.

The women's exposed butts deconstruct the political world with its moral decadence and very little regard for the citizens' aspirations.

Parodying Transformations

The stylistics of Ngugi's naming in *Wizard of the Crow* combines cultural ethics with burlesque nomenclature, depending on the character's role in the text's thematic while the integration of Rabelaisian aesthetics in Ngugi's nomenclature represents his critical perception of historical transformation. In the same way that Labou Tansi's (anti)hero suffers from the speech malady of *palilalia* in *L'Etat Honteux* (*The Shameful State*), the power hungry characters in *Wizard of the Crow* are all stuck by the unexpressed racial wishes of becoming white men. As seen earlier in the case of Tajirika, they suffer from the "if" malady and have to be 'cured' by the Wizard of the Crow who induces them release the magic word, their ultimate wish. This humorous parody is reminiscent of Bakhtin's narration of a stuttering incidence in Schneegans' *commerdia dell'arte*:

A stutterer talking with Harlequin cannot pronounce a difficult word; he makes a great effort, loses his breath, keeping the word down his throat, sweats and gapes, trembles, chokes. His face is swollen, his eyes pop; "Finally Harlequin, weary of waiting, relieves the stutterer by surprise; he rushes ahead and forward, and hits the man in the abdomen. The difficult word is born at last. (304)

Re-echoed in several passages in *Wizard of the Crow* in which Kamiti attempts to cure each and every member of the political leadership, this humorous aesthetics provides a clue to the understanding of the name of the absurd Republic of A-b-u-r-i-r-i-a. As we noted above, a name in Ngugi's fiction is not a mere noun, it is an event, a process and a narrative. It is through the analogy of stuttering and the complex historical *narrative* it distends that we analyze the name: A-B-U-R-I-R-I-A. The setting of Ngugi's baroque text cannot be pinned down to any specific geographical locality. We are only told that 'Aburiria'[4] is found somewhere in the continent of Africa. As a form of geographical designation, it is evanescent and indeterminate. However, on the basis of its morphology, it could be considered a narrative summary of the plot and a critique of political transformation. 'A-b-u-r-i-r-i-a' suggests a process of revolution, a major event B (a plosive sound which phonetically marks a change) that moves history from its primordial condition A, raising immense hope and euphoria, captured by the high vowel sound [u]. This plosive event that signals progression unfortunately dithers on a form of con-fusion given that the *eu*phoria is followed by a series of repetitive and degenerative glides [r] and the low *dis*phoric vowel [i]. Given the recurrence of the glides [r-r-] and the corresponding low vowel [i-i-], could we talk of an insinuation of Mbembe's view of the stuttering movement of African history? Is the relationship between the two occurrences A - B to be represented as continuity instead of the great break that it purports? However, the specter of the initial and near deterministic [A] which reappears as the ultimate point (this time in small letter) threatens the movement with reversion or regression. It is at this interval that the process of trans-formation can be said to conceal a regressive element.

The above analysis symbolizes the influence of historical determinism on *Wizard of the Crow* and the tendency of the Ruler's so-called progress to signify regression into new forms of slavery/colonialism. Could the name of Ngugi's fictional Republic (with its inherent synecdoche of reference) therefore be a critique against the re-colonization of Africa? We would push this formalistic analysis further by using Hayden White's model for the representation of historical events in historical/literary narratives. As quoted in Leitch, White shows how history and literature both plot series of events (a b c d e…n.) in a variety of schemata:

-A^5 b c d e …n/ a B c d e …n/ a b C d e…n/ a b c D e…n/ a b c d E...n (1546)

White argues that it is in the plotting of history along such schemata that various forms of determinisms and ideologies are observed ranging from the totemic A in Freud, Marx, and Rousseau to the romantic E of Augustinian's millenarian *City of God* and Hegelian Idealism in the *Philosophy of History.* (1547). If we plot Ngugi's Republic of A-b-u-r-i-r-i-a and the historiology of its fictional world, we would arrive at the first structure above: with the seminal /A/ and the movement towards the /a/. Assuming that the ultimate /a/ in "Aburiria" would represent the /e/ in this schema would lead us to the risk of reductive (mis)reading of the text. It is for this reason that the /a/ could be problematized to *also* denote the possibility of a new beginning, the openness of the future to a variety of unpredictable possibilities. But the miniscule nature of the /a/ entails that the new future would not come in a Big Bang but through progressive work, individual and communal consciousness. It is the controversy of this /a/ and the uncertain nature of the beginning it heralds that situates Ngugi's fable within the ambits of the modern novel with its symbolic indeterminacy and ambiguous ending, epitomized on the one hand by Tajirika's seizure of power and the growing consciousness of Eldoret by the Movement for the voice of the people, on the other. *Wizard of the Crow* is therefore caught in between Augustinian Romantic determinism and Beckettan representation of Fallen Man. The novel therefore ends in a polyphonic mode with elements of the resurgence of civic consciousness amidst the perpetuation of dictatorship by Tajirika.

The representation of this 'problematic echo of transformation' engages our analysis of (re-) naming in the public sphere. Though the end of the Cold war signals the advent of democracy and the advent of multiparty politics, the leadership in Wizard turn these ideals into a sham. The democracy to which the Ruler 'gives birth' at the end of the narrative is a smoke screen. Power circulates in the hands of successive members of the ruling class. In a pompous inauguration of the putatively 'new era' which he claims to have initiated, the Ruler remains synonymous to the State:

He would be the normal head of all political parties. This meant that in the next general elections, all parties would, of course, be choosing him as their candidate for the presidency: His victory would be a victory for all the parties, and more important for Aburirians, a victory for the wise and tested leadership[...] Direct Democracy. Open Democracy. Baby D is born. (699)

The democratic transition is guided by the self-interests of the Ruler. The 'Ruler's party' is merely transformed into the 'Ruling party,' auguring no substantial change for the country and its process of democratization. In fact, those who form the opposition are former members of the stagnant political system who later return to the political scene as simulated opposition. One such example is Sikiokku, the former Security Secretary and close aid of the Ruler, who creates an "opposition party", the "Loyal Democratic Party" as he pledges loyalty to the Ruler.

Ngugi's text inertly questions the concept of transformation as progress from oppression to freedom, from war to peace in the representation of the historical moments/movements of the 1990s. To examine temporality in *Wizard of the Crow* from the Cold War perspective is to perceive the "wind of change" with even more rigorous skepticism than the preceding wave of independence. Ngugi recaptures the complexities of African political field in the late eighties and early nineties. Even though certain civic rights are achieved, the eventful 1990 marks the beginning of an open-ended moment where new positions of power/subalternity are re-negotiated and former dictatorships devise new ways of survival. The gains of multiparty, civil society are threatened by new forms of hegemonic control: 'corporonialism' (747), the extraversion of governance by transnational and multinational co-operations. When Nyawira tells Kamiti that her boss, Tajirika has a very important "reception dinner in honour of the mission from the GB", Kamiti seems confused: "GB? Great Britain?" Kamiti asked, a little puzzled. What was she talking about and what did it have to do with her setting up an appointment? "Not Great Britain! Global Bank!" (51).

The emphatic "No" and the confusion in the acronym 'GB' is both satirical and ironic. When considered within Ngugi's anti-imperialist tradition this affirmative "No" is an epathonorsis (a 'calculated error') that conflates both 'Great Britain' and 'Global Bank.' It summarizes the history of global capitalism from the era of British imperial mercantilism to modern neo-liberalism. In other words, 'GB' underlines the palimpsest of the present moment of trans-formation. Partly due to internal protests and the pressure of Ambassador Gabriel Gemstone,[6] the Ruler is forced to 'democratize.' With the end of the Cold War, he will no more use the trump card of the "war against communism" as a pretext to hunt down his detractors whom he indexes as 'Communists' and 'Anarchists.'

Despite his satirical portrayal of the moralist connotation of 'civil society' and 'international community,' Ngugi represents the post-1990 public sphere not as a stage of unilateral/ monopolistic discourse but as one in which hegemonic naming and meaning formation are negotiated and contested by a growing civil society. The names attached to particular social and national events define the interpellation of subject in the public and private spheres, soliciting participation, complacency and collaboration. The public sphere in Ngugi's text becomes a venue for the contestation of State 'ordained' symbols and meanings. In consonance with our prior analogy of the State's appropriation of the word/ culture/ world, Achille Mbembe posits that the post-colonial State:

Claims to hold the truth with regard to Africa and its history, to codify it, to demarcate, unify and divide space. The Theologian State is one which does not only arrogate the distribution of power and influence, social relations, economic arrangements and political processes. It also constitutes itself into the instituting principle behind the language and myths of a given society) *(my translation)* (Mbembe 128).[7]

In Ngugi's imaginary world, the constituted subject does not obsequiously ingest the State's design of meaning formation, but attempts to subvert, re-signify and rename it. When the Ruler celebrates the 'Birth of Baby Democracy,' the official connotation is overturned by the Movement for the Voice of the people. The movement calls it: Day of National Renewal (669), underlining the capacity of the people to reclaim their culture of unity in the struggle for representation. It brings out the fact that the postcolonial public sphere is a space of negotiation and contention of national symbols, metaphors and frames of meaning construction. The two forms of metaphors are thereby confronted in the public sphere. In the same way as Guy Debord's analogy of the 'armed faith'(137) of 'colonial missionaries', State discourse also operates in the form of 'armed metaphors' since the State often resorts to State ideological and repressive apparatuses for its *en-forcement*. However, with the moment of change, the Ruler's control over the army becomes uncertain. In this dimension, the progressive outlook of Ngugi's text can be highlighted. When the State orders the military to fire at the protesters, a boomerang effect is created "The two main pillars on which his rule depended, the armed forces and the West, had loosened considerably" (645).

Ngugi's representation of the political and economic present of post-colonialism entails explicit narrative choices in his depiction of the capitalist project of the State and the neoliberal system. When Ngugi's narrative encounters intricate analysis of economy, the nature of expression and the logic of analysis spill out of the hand of the metadiegetic narrator and gives way to what could be the implied author's voice. This is evident towards the end of the text, when the narrator defines the logic of modern neo-liberalism as it affects the citizens of the Republic of Aburiria. The new capitalist system is indicted as 'corporonialism', underlying the pervasive influence of transnational corporations on the neo-colony: "We would volunteer Aburiria to become the first to be wholly managed by private capital, to become the first voluntary corporate colony, a corporony, the first in the new global order" (746-747). The preoccupation with economy and the parody of the capitalist status of the Aburirian economy reveal the multivocality and polyphony of Ngugi's text.

The main narrator, Arigaigai Gathere, the half-educated police, near aphasiac constable at the origin of the whole saga of the Wizard of the Crow, more often engages in economic analyses that slow down the tempo of the narrative and creates a form of dissonance with the overall burlesque tonality of the text. In *Wizard of the Crow*, there is therefore a struggle between the traditional storytelling model which is at the basis of the *Gicaandi* narrator and the overarching political intentionality of the author. In the same manner as Ngugi's hero, Ngugi's narrator is a loaded narrator, overburdened with historical memory of imperialism and most importantly, the memory of Ngugi's earlier works. The voice of the author therefore competes with that of the narrator with the former's tendency to analyze processes, direct readership, indulge into invectives and to qualify and evaluate what is narrated through a system of judgmental adjectivisation. This is brought out in the following passage: "When the farmer and the manufacturer grow and make things within, the neo-imperial class imports en masse the cheapest from abroad and undermine the efforts within. We live in a corporate globe under imperial corporonialism, as proudly claimed by the new ogres" (760).

In conclusion, it can be said that one of the major conflicts in Ngugi's text circulates around the question of naming. The system of naming in *Wizard of the Crow* characterizes the question of self-awareness, friction between State and society, the tensions within movements of change and more importantly, the various tendencies, temperaments and tonalities within Ngugi's authorial consciousness. Across the breadth of Ngugi's literary career, naming has often been a major paradigm of representation and a gateway into his metaphorical system. Names do not denote the solitary individual in their existential present-moment but relates them to society and history. The name entrusts characters with a mission, and accords them place and function in the community. The name of a character, just like that of a setting is often a carrier of a historical memory and a cultural identity. It is the name that brings the character into being and re-defines their relationship with the outside world, enhancing their self-realization and their reconciliation with the community in a spirit of collective agency and the crystallization of a communal spirit in the quest for social change.

Chapter 7

Proverbs in Ojaide's Contexts

S B Ekundayo

Proverbs are the palm oil with which words are eaten.
- Chinua Achebe

PROVERBS and aphorisms are related figurative ways of using language in Africa. Achebe's novels not only popularised their use in African fiction but encrusted them as integral attributes of African cultural locution. Aphorism may include proverbs because proverbs themselves are aphorismic. In fact, most proverbs are aphorisms but not all aphorisms may pass for proverbs. Some other terms for *aphorism* are *maxim, precept, apothegm, wit*, etc. In strict context we may establish a nuance between aphorism and proverb. Aphorisms come more directly than proverbs. They are usually short, devoid of elaborate analogies, comparisons or symbolisms characteristic of proverbs. Aphorisms are striking phrases and statements that convey truth, wisdom and humour. They are analogous to epigrams in poetry, but shorter in form. Some examples of aphorisms in Nigerian society are 'men will always be men,' 'no condition is permanent,' 'heaven helps those who help themselves,' 'to become a man is not easy,' 'the truth is bitter, but we must say it,' etc.

Proverbs, on the other hand, come "in more or less fixed form marked by shortness, sense and salt distinguished by the popular acceptance of the truth tersely expressed in it" (Finnegan 393). They often contain metaphors and symbolisms, analogies and wits. They have deeper structures and meanings extracted from the surface structures than mere aphorismic statements, reflecting "old-age wisdom" many of them being "rhetorical, humorous and imagistic" (Akporoaro 110).

African story telling consists of creating literary characters or human beings in a work, giving them roles and human or inhuman attributes. Characters in African stories may thus be human, animal, spirits and even non-living things. Several ways exist for delineating literary characters. Abrams summarizes them to two ways. These are "showing" and "telling". In showing, the writer presents the characters in their actions and behaviours to the audience or readers to pass their judgment. In telling, the writer personally comments on the characters, exposing their natures and personalities (33-4). Murphy identifies a number of ways in which characterization is done. These are through: "personal description, character as seen by another, comments of the author, the past life of the character as presented in the work, conversation of others, the characters' reactions to issues and events, what the characters themselves say, soliloquy and spoken thoughts (161-173).

To analyse Ojaides's proverbs, we must take into account some theories and concepts about proverb use: (i) the cognitive approach with reference to the theories of "proverb as a species of metaphor," and "proverb as an analogical, problem-solving model;" (ii) the ethnographic/ anthropological theory which sees "proverb as folklore and performance-based"; (iii) the integrative approach, which is a combination of the good sides of different theories; and (iv) African (writers') concept of proverbs as an integral way of life and expression of being.

The cognitive theory is concerned with how the human mind receives, processes and interprets proverbs. "Proverbs as species of metaphor" and "proverb as analogy" theories are of the cognitive approach. Lakoff and Turner argue that a series of metaphors and images that reflect concepts condition our thinking and mind at a deep subconscious level. They say that proverbs are more or less poems to be interpreted. Like other metaphors, proverbs make readers/ listeners identify a "source domain" and match the source domain with "the target domain" which the context of use may give or not give. A source domain is the area or occupation of life from where the proverb is formed and the target domain is the area to which meaning is imposed. Accordingly, four basic tools assist the audience of a proverb to reconcile the source domain with the target domain to derive the contextual meaning. These are "the generic is specific", "the concept of the Great Chain of Being", "the nature of things" and "the principle of verbal economy and the maxim of quantity." The generic is specific means that reference to images and metaphors have a specific source just as the intended target domain is specific or specified. The concept of the Great Chain of Being relates to our collective unconscious, the sets of beliefs we inherited, which assist us in understanding our world, our language and expressing ourselves. These two combine with our universal knowledge of the nature of things, how things work, the arrangement of nature, etc and lastly with verbal economy and the maxim of quantity, at which level we can separate what is relevant from what is irrelevant to extract meanings (167).

An example they use to illustrate these four tools of proverb interpretation is

Ants on millstone
Whichever way they walk
They go round with it

The source domain is the world of ants on a millstone. The target domain is not quite specified. It is left for the listener to interpret or identify. The Great Chain of Being stimulates us to see what ants are and what they could stand for and their place in the ecosystem. The principle of verbal economy makes us avoid unnecessary details about ants and millstones. Practical knowledge of the nature of things enables us to see that ants by nature are small creatures and that a millstone rolls. So, the movement of ants on a millstone does not affect the millstone. Rather, the rolling of the millstone controls the movement of the ants.

On the other hand, Honeck asserts that cultural context enrich the study of proverbs, although he does not emphasize the cultural context but says that proverbs can be taken away from the cultural specifics since "the mental structures and processes of the *Homo sapiens* are explainable on the basis of theoretical principles" (37). He argues, against this backdrop, that proverbs are not poems to be interpreted but problem to be solved in a face-to-face situation. Honeck's theory presumes two cognitive contexts for proverb use: "the irrelevant" and "the relevant." In the first context, the listener is given only the source domain. S/he is then left to determine the target domain. In the irrelevant context, going by Honeck and Temple's example, a listener runs into a proverb or vice versa "out of the blues." For example, a stranger in an elevator or lift tells another stranger: "A net with a hole in it won't catch any fish" (68). Or on the street, a stranger tells a stranger "Not every oyster contains a pearl" (128). Invariably, the stranger tries attempts to interpret the proverb in different ways. Since the usage may not be amenable to literal interpretation at the level of physical oyster, s/he moves to the literary level and applies his knowledge of the nature of things, oyster and pearls to extract meanings that could apply. That oyster could be pearl-less is given or taken for granted, and so irrelevant, but the relevant thing is the essence and intention of the proverb. If the street user of this proverb intends a specific meaning, he may have to supply the clue which becomes "the conceptual base" of the proverb. The speaker may display a scratched useless lottery card to his addressee, which then explains the proverb. Honeck and Temple later add the concept of "the cognitive ideals," which they use to explain the opposing, binary nature of proverbs, the ideal and the otherwise, the imperfect nature of things. Ideally, oysters should contain pearls, but sometimes, they do not.

In this way proverbs become abstractions that can be interpreted by theoretical rules, not necessarily as culture-situation based: "The fact that proverbs can be created anew is important theoretically because it makes it clear that individual proverbs do not have to be part of the linguistic heritage of a culture" (99) as "minds operate by universal principles" (218).

Honeck's conclusion is questionable and so is Lakoff's and Turner's. Bradbury and Arora, among many other scholars who propose either the integrative or the ethnographic/ anthropological approach, have criticized the strands of theories in the cognitive approach. Bradbury is of the view that Lakoff and Turner "do not inquire into the context that produce their *Asian Figures"* just as Honeck shows "little concern about the sources of his examples."

When we turn to evidence from Middle Ages (or if we were to examine an existing society where proverbs use is culturally central), we meet strong tradition-bearers, those who hold a repertoire of proverbs in memory and use then, in ways not accounted for by either theory....

Both cognitive theories focus their attention almost exclusively on the intellectual gymnastics of innocent bystanders accosted by proverbs. But familiarity with the living traditions studied by ethnographers or the once-living tradition depicted in Chaucer's fiction compels us to ask also about the mental activity involved in proverb production. Who are these people in Honeck's theory who pop into elevators and utter proverbs? How do they come up with proverbs? Why do they use them? (274-5)

Similarly, Mieder argues that proverbs are of the folk: "A proverb is a short, generally known sentence of the folk which contains wisdom, truth, morals and traditional views in a metaphorical, fixed and memorizable form and which is handed down from generation to generation" (24). He has established in various works that proverbs are culture-based, comes in a number of figurative and imagistic ways and the rich cultural legacies of diverse peoples of the world. For Africans and African writers proverbs and their uses transcend theories and intellectual hair splitting. Africans live in a world of proverbs, and this reality reflects in their works. Mieder rightly says that West Africa has the richest stock of proverbs in the world (108) and African writers have amply shown this in their works. Achebe's conceptualization of proverb as "the palm oil with which words are eaten" (5) should be taken seriously because it is laden with meanings. Examining the aesthetics of proverbs in African fiction, Osani notes:

The African proverb is a distinctive aspect of the use of language employed mainly by adults in informal conversations as well in formal speeches at meetings, conferences and other occasions. In Nigeria, proverbs appear in literature -whether traditional or modern- and in other arts, especially music. They have been demonstrably used by Nigerian writers in poetry, drama and prose fiction not only to project the cultural values of the people, but more importantly, to also achieve aesthetic effect. (95)

We submit that it is more practically and intellectually rewarding to integrate all the strengths of various theories without their weaknesses. Proverbs, first all, belong to a people, a tradition and culture, and they are handed down from generation to generation as metaphoric, symbolic or aphorismic representations. Writers or speakers, being members of the society of proverbs, then use them in their works and speeches. Thereafter, the hearers' processes of cognition take over to interpret them, the hearers also being members of the society.

II

Proverbs in Ojaide's Works

The use of proverbs is a major distinguishing narrative style of African novels. It is difficult to read an African/ Nigerian novel without running into strings of proverbs and aphorisms because the artful and apt use of proverbs is a remarkable and distinguishing characteristic of oratory, orators and general interaction in traditional African settings. Quite often, Nigerian novelists lace or sprinkle their narratives with proverbs which enhance the telling of their tales. From the pioneer novelists like Achebe to recent ones like Ojaide, the use of proverbs has remained one of the hallmarks of the genres. In the words of Uyo,

> the use of proverbs shows conversational eloquence and ...sayings are usually learnt from listening to elders... Proverbs can be used in several ways to teach moral lessons, influence people...and to entertain. A number of Nigerian prose writers are exceptionally skillful in the creative use of proverbs in their works of fiction....the creative use of figurative language is one of the greatest achievements of the author and this makes the novel interesting to read even as a narrative about contemporary issues.(6)

Similarly, Ogunjimi and N'Allah recognise in proverbs "the ingredients of harmonizing the life rhythm of any community" (65). Thus the use of proverbs betrays the *Africanness* of the writers and projects the settings and thematic preoccupations of their works. According to Jegede,

> Proverbs speak louder than words... Proverbs form a pool of linguistic and thematic resources from which speakers and writers...have drawn...
> The functions of proverbs as means of embellishing speech and performance, projecting the business sense of a people, portraying the image of a community and preserving the history and culture of a people are usually reflected in literary works. (35-6)

As a writer Ojaide "engages metaphors, images, linguistic and semantic manipulations and legends from folktales and history to speak his thoughts, make his points and depict topical issues" (Olaofioye 7). His works are animated through "communal landscape given in myth, folklore and common histories that provide a community with a source of identity" (Okuyade 24). Carruth acknowledges that Ojaide is "supple, strong, various, colourful, moving and invariably interesting" (qtd. in Olaofioye 105). Ojaide himself admits that the poet seems to be translating from local language to English (67). Indeed, literal translations and renditions of local languages and structures permeate Ojaide's creative works. In the same literary tradition, Ojaide consciously infuses his novel with proverbs that enrich his narrative.

Matters of the Moment is set in the 1990s Nigeria during the heydays of military rule. Dede, the hero, is a journalist trained in the United States of America. He returns to Nigeria brimming with principles and ideologies for change. However, his marriage is cut short by a dirty divorce case. Franka, his divorced wife, becomes a socialite who uses her femininity to influence highly placed men and climb the corridors of power. There is a reversal of fortune when General Ogiso, the military head of state dies in strange circumstances. The trend of events yokes the divorced couple in crisis and together they unseat a military tyrant.

There are approximately fifteen proverbs in the novel. The first is right in the opening paragraph of the narrative. When Franka, the heroine, meets Dede, the hero, whom she believes is her 'Mr Right,' the author uses a proverb to reveal and concretize the feelings of the characters and also foreshadows the imminence of a love affair and possibly marriage between them: "When the ripe cherry fruit finds its favourite, it falls freely for the chosen one to pick" (6). The use of this proverb gives readers insight into the thinking and expectation of Franka Udi.

In another example, in his unpublished poem, Dede refers to General Ogiso as "the leopard" whose "anger could only be appeased with blood" (34). The full form of this proverb in local usage and in folktales is: 'Only blood can appease the rage of a leopard.' This proverb, which clearly delineates Ogiso as a tyrant, is also a warning that Dede will pay dearly for it should he publish the poem. So he keeps the poem till a more auspicious time.

Somewhere in the narrative, Ode, one of the major characters, is hesitant to enter into another marriage, having failed in his first marriage. This experience is captured in an apt proverb: "One who already had a cold from one divorce could get pneumonia from a second one" (67). In this context, we see that he has misgivings about another marriage and so is hesitant and cautious, reminding us of the English aphorism, 'once beaten, twice shy.' Similarly, when Franka falls in love for the second time with Chief Ugbo, she observes that an "animal that had escaped from a trap avoids an arced stick". Was the same caution not exercised by a fish that had struggled out of hook in avoiding whatever metal-held bait it came across?" (88). The underlying message here is that divorce or broken home can generate apathy and misgivings for marriage. In characterization, it shows Franka gaining in psychological maturity and experience, and foretells the change Franka will soon begin to exhibit in love affairs.

Again, Furu, a female character who has not had a relationship for a time is likened to an uncultivated piece of land. Commenting on her prolonged single status, her mother says: "A fallow field needs to be cultivated." Her mother reinforces this with yet another proverb that states an empty market invites spirits. Here the necessity of being in a relationship or marriage is underscored. A mature person without a stable relationship is vulnerable to all manner of things: loneliness, heartache, social abuse, loss of self-confidence, childlessness, etc. These are some of the evil spirits that invade an empty market.

After undergoing a second heartbreak, Franka vows with the following aphorism: "If men had to be men, she had to be a woman" (96). We see Franka's resolve to begin a kind of life in the use of this proverb. Men constantly have affairs with women and then walk away. In the same vein, she will henceforth chase after her own interest too. Subsequently, in a newspaper article, we meet Dede saying: everybody wants to go to heaven but does not want to die. This adaptation from popular Caribbean reggae lyrics of the eighties is used to show people's general love and desire for a good society, riches and the sweet things of life. Unfortunately, however, people are often not willing and ready to pay the supreme price.

Franka thinks of 'microwaving' a degree in law through illegal means and sharp practices and at the same time reflects on the consequences of treading such a path. She fears that she may not be able to practise with a law degree acquired with the microwave of sharp practices, and that will be disgraceful in the end. This spectre is captured in the proverb that states "the wind would blow feathers off the fowl's behind and everyone would see the eyesore." Its symbolic note is if she bribes her way through school, her mediocrity and counterfeit degree would be exposed during practice in court. The quintessence of Ojaide's proverbs emerges on page 148 of the novel where the author drops a cluster to accentuate a very important point:

One cannot allow the leopard and its cubs to terrorize the land. Let other animals use their wits to bring down their tormentor. The small bird animals that are possible victims of the leopard could catch the monstrous animal asleep and deal it a death blow. If all fowls are united, the hawk would not succeed in snatching a single one away. It is only when broomsticks are tied together that they sweep clean.

With this, Ojaide mobilizes his audience and reinforces his clarion call for a united action against evil and oppression. The theme being stressed by the use of these proverbs is the need for unity, the power of tact and unity. Elsewhere Dede likens the people's lethargy, inertia and complacence to the scenario of "the angry dog" which "has been given a sop and its bark and bite are gone back to sleep" (100). In this proverb, Ojaide invokes the tradition of resisting injustice and corruption in Nigeria -the setting of the novel. Like angry dogs, people bark loudly as if they could really bite. But once they are offered 'kola' or government appointment, etc., they turn their eyes the other way, sleeping and snoring while society deteriorates. Franka Udi all along has been avoiding Dede, her estranged husband. However, her game of hide-and-seek culminates in her running to Dede toward the end of the novel. This experience is wrapped in the aphorism of someone fleeing from death who ironically finds death squatting in front of her in her so-called hideout or refuge. (181). Franka finds Dede standing before her in her most exigent moment. Dede against whom she is imbued with the passions of vengeance is now on the person to save her from the mob.

The use of proverbs and aphorisms in *Matters of the Moment* underscores an artistic development that makes the narrative interesting and evocative. These proverbs reinforce the subject-matter of human vice, the social scourge of a broken home, the challenges of divorce and single parenthood, and the spectacle of vengeance, oppression and bad governance in Africa. Besides, these proverbs put a stamp of *Africanness* on Ojaide's narrative, revealing the socio-cultural peculiarities of its environment.

Chapter 8

Igbo Traditional Morality

E Ezedike

AT some point in the development of societies, demands arose for the control of destructive passions of humans -demands for honesty and transparency, for the sanctity of human life, and for justice and orderliness. These were necessary conditions to promote the well-being of society and ensure the peaceful co-existence of all members. Moreover, society needed such moral rules for the protection of individuals against the tendencies toward injustice and oppression by others. Rules of conduct, thus, became quite indispensable and imperative for the survival of the group. With the emergence of civil societies and modern governments, relevant and elaborate moral codes and positive laws were developed and imposed.

In Africa, however, this development has seen the transmutation of traditional morality which has continued to decline in relevance to the contemporary mind (Ezedike 1). Western concepts of morality, with its predatory influence on African culture, have had far reaching negative effects. Traditional morality appears to have lost intrinsic importance in the African mind. With the deplorable moral state of affairs in Africa, nay, world over, created by westernisation, especially with its de-emphasis of the traditional (a term that appears mutually exclusive with modernity), we need to revisit the past in order to investigate and unearth the primordial affirmation of the truth about our moral heritage with a new appreciation of its worth and role in traditional African society. It is this "realignment to the indigenous harmonic traditions of ancient ways of being -which has been the original trajectory of African familial, and cultural existence" (Ce and Smith 10) that might enable us to develop conceptual paradigms and a strong ethical content for modernization -a kind of "cultural renaissance and ethical renewal" (Kigongo 2). Igbo traditional society will serve as a case study of traditional African morality and a platform for the ideal of cultural complementarity as enunciated by a few scholars.

Tradition and Morality

As to the question: "whence does morality derive its norms, the force of its demand and sanction?" the answers have been various. There are those who hold that morality has its origin in society; that is, it is essentially a social phenomenon. For society to keep alive and its machinery running smoothly, it evolves a system of self-preservation. Thus the sense of "ought" which resides within each person is a result of this system which society created. Others have told us that what we call morality is little more than a product of common sense.

In order to live, man must adapt himself to his environment. Experience soon taught him what could be done and what must be avoided. A steady accumulation of this experience over time has resulted in a very strong sense of what has come to be popularly known as "right and wrong".

Traditional moral values in the Igbo nation include what the people prefer as well as what they find important and morally right or wrong. It refers to "a set of institutionalized ideals which guide and direct the patterns of life of Africans" (Sogolo 119). It is a collective conception of norms, and standards which act as the charter for acceptable conduct in the society (Ozumba 198). Moral values are essentially referential: every moral value is a value for someone and thus relative. This is not because what is morally good for Africa is necessarily unwholesome for Europe, but rather because a moral value has its *raison d'etre* in its original context of relevance, its initial *locus standi,* from where it can have or acquire universal validity (Esomonu 119). This implies that on the account of their acceptability and usefulness, moral values can be universally applied for the benefit of every human society.

In all, morality in Igbo thought could be seen to be in an intimate relationship with the ontological order of the African universe. The order is 'given', if not explicitly God-given. It is believed that any infraction of this order is a contradiction in life and brings about a physical disorder which reveals the fault (Shorter 62). This implies a vital link between ontology and morality. Breaking the moral code is seen as being capable of upsetting the ontological order of the universe which can attract serious divine sanctions for the whole community. Thus, there is nothing like personal morality in African traditional ethic because whatever morality that exists is shared by all (Ozumba 57). This is informed by the Igbo proverb that says: "if one finger brought oil, it soiled the others" (Achebe 114). Hence, to keep the whole fingers clean (that is to be morally upright), the people endeavour to conform to the moral code of the community in order to be in harmony with the ontological order of universe. They are strongly convinced of the repercussions of evil acts since they "are capable of vitiating the experience of transcendent complementary unity of consciousness that binds all realities together" (Asouzu 174). It would, therefore, be improper to dismiss traditional approaches to morality as emotive, irrational or non-analytical as some positivists do. Also, we would not be saying the whole truth by claiming that traditional ethic is essentially a religious ethic. Since ethical rules have implications that are not only supernaturalistic but also humanistic, we should, therefore, view traditional morality from a perspective that is devoid of undue or excessive supernaturalism.

The pursuit and practice of moral virtue are intrinsic to the conception of person within traditional African ontology (Gyekye 109). The actions of an individual, good or bad, affect other aspects of reality in as much as an individual exists as part of the whole ontological system. With this ontological nexus, an individual can destabilize the moral order through indulgence in certain actions or inactions that are inimical to the ontological equilibrium. This makes punishment for any infraction of the moral code inevitable.

Crime and Punishment

Succinctly put, crimes are harmful conducts or omissions that are prohibited, on threatened sanctions, by the laws of the state (Curzon 11). In Igboland a crime is a harmful conduct or omission of individuals in violation of the moral code (*Omenala*), which has injurious consequences for whole the society. Distinction is made between those offences which are "Nso or Aru" (abomination) and those which are not (Uchendu. 42). Of the perpetrator of the former offence it would be said: "*Omeruru ala*" (He polluted the land). When a man commits a crime against the established order, he incurs the wrath and punishment of the deities. If the crime was manifest in the external form, the culprit faces public sanctions, which sometimes could include death, a heavy fine, banishment or ostracism from the rest of the society until the offender is cleansed through appropriate rituals of atonement.

The foregoing leads to the concept of punishment which, simply put, is a penalty imposed on someone for violating moral or legal rules. According to Ozumba: "Punishment simplistically can be defined as an act of inflicting varying degrees of pain or suffering on someone because of what he/she has done which is considered as evil" (58). For Iwe, it is "a form of deprivation extrinsically attached to a human act of commission or omission perceived as anti-social or a violation of established norms and values of a given society" (245). Sterba, from the moral point of view, says that "punishment is hardship involving moral condemnation and denunciation inflicted on a person who is found guilty of an offence by someone entitled to do so" (244). This definition of punishment distinguishes it from mere "jungle justice". According to Hart: "Punishment must involve pain or other consequences morally considered unpleasant; it must be for an offence against legal rules; it is inflicted on an actual or supposed offender for his offence, it must be intentionally administered by a human being" (66). Hart limits the administration of punishment to "a human being" and to the exclusion of divine punishments. This appears to be a narrow view of the subject. The same thing applies to Black's definition of punishment as any fine, penalty, or confinement inflicted upon a person by the authority of the law and the judgment and sentence of the court, for some crime or offence committed by him for his omission of a duty enjoined by law (110). Generally speaking, punishment could be retributive or deterrent. The retributive theory holds that that when a crime is committed, the balance of social and moral order is upset. Thus the only way to restore equilibrium and justice is to mete out a commensurate punishment to the culprit. On the other hand, the deterrent theory holds that punishment should be imposed on offenders to reduce future infractions of the law.

For the Igbo, punishment could serve both retributive and deterrent purposes depending on the nature of crime. In Esomonu words, "belief in divine moral code and the ability of the gods to punish any deviation from or violations of the divine law was and is the most powerful mechanism of societal control in Igbo society" (183). According to Mbiti, Africans have a strong sense retributive punishment: "The majority of African people believe that God punishes in this life. Thus, he is concerned with the moral life of mankind and therefore upholds the moral law" (210). Mbiti further elaborates that with a few exceptions, there is no belief that a person is punished in the hereafter for what he does wrong in this life. When punishment comes, it comes in the present life. For that reason, misfortunes may be interpreted as indicating that the sufferer has broken some moral or ritual conduct against God, the spirits, the elders or other members of the society. This does not contradict the belief that certain misfortunes are the clandestine work of some mischievous members of the society, like sorcerers and witches, against their fellow men. One writer observes that "the gods were interested in the moral probity or impropriety of the individual members of the tribe. It was firmly believed that any serious lapse might be punished by the gods" (Nduka 106). And another points out that the community was always anxious to see that the metaphysical disequilibrium would not result from commission of crimes or violation of divinely formulated moral codes which embraced every aspect of moral behaviour as authenticated by priests and elders - the conservatories of tradition and of the wisdom of the land (Esomonu 183).

For the Igbo, therefore, punishment serves as a veritable weapon for protecting society's moral values from flagrant disregard and decay. The same might be said about many other African peoples. There is, indeed, the strong belief in divine and societal punishment. In Igbo traditional society, *Omenala* (customs and moral codes) provide sanctions against violators and those considered to be dangerous to the entire community. The standard of conduct among them was expressed in unwritten form and the forbidden acts were recognized and punished as transgression against traditions and mores. This becomes necessary when crime poses a serious threat to whole society. Therefore, it is the desire of the Igbo that evil perpetrators be punished in order to avert a collective punishment.

Every community in Africa has its own forms of punishment for various offences on both legal and moral issues. Mbiti remarks that these range from death for offences like sorcery, witchcraft, murder and adultery to fines of cattle, sheep or money for minor cases like accidental injury to one's companion or damage to neighbours' fields (211). Human punishment, as Mbiti puts it, is understood as the "action of the society against one who has transgressed its laws and so threatened the common good" (211). Indeed, all traditional African societies knit together by laws and customs, lay claim to and exercise the right of punishing violators of such codes of conduct because they are necessary for the well-being of the society.

(i) Murder - The Igbo regard human life as very sacred. Murder is included in one of the prohibitions of *"Omenala"* called *"Nso ala"* or abomination. The prohibition portrays an entrenched respect for the sanctity

of human life. "Implicit in this prohibition is the realization that human life is sacred of and by itself, apart from any profitable function it may serve, as a tool of "productivity" (Esomonu 186). In many parts of Igboland, the punishment for wilful murder is death by hanging. The houses and properties of the whole family are equally destroyed. Occasionally, a murderer may act cowardly by running from the village. In that case, he must remain in exile until the bitterness subsides. Should any of the deceased's relation see him return to the village without adequate propitiation, they could kill him on sight. In the case of accidental murder like that of Okonkwo in *Things Fall Apart*, the crime carried the penalty of banishment and destruction of everything he had acquired (86, 87). Punishment in the two cases is meant to appease the goddess of the earth (ala) and to serve as a deterrent to others. As Vallenga observes:

> Even from time immemorial the conviction of good society has been that life is sacred and he who violates the sacredness of human life through murder, must pay supreme penalty just because it is sacred. The law of capital punishment must stand as a silent but powerful witness of sacredness of God given life, which can be shown only, through the administration of active justice, when the sacredness of human life is violated through crimes. (129)

Here capital punishment for murder seems morally justifiable and because of the sacredness of human life. This argument for the death penalty seems plausible as it goes a long way as Iroegbu would say, in checkmating the *homo lupus homini* (man is wolf to man) tendency in the society (381).

(ii) Suicide - Suicide has been defined by Sheidman as "the human act of self-inflicted, self-intentioned cessation" (229). Suicide is a manifestation of the most extreme and arbitrary self-assertion of spite and desperation. It is common belief among the Igbo that life belongs to God ("Chi-nwe-ndu"). For an individual to wilfully terminate his/ her life would imply arrogating to oneself a prerogative that solely belongs to God. Hence such heinous "*Aru*" (crime) desecrates the land. For them, it is an aberration, an act contrary to the deepest instinct of nature -the instinct of self-preservation. In his dialogue, *Laws,* Plato condemns suicide saying:

But what of him who takes [his own life]? I mean the man whose violence frustrates the decree of destiny by self-slaughter though no sentence of the state has required this of him, no stress of cruel and inevitable calamity driven him to the act, and he has involved in no desperate and intolerable disgrace, the man who thus gives unrighteous sentence against himself from mere poltroonery and unmanly cowardice. (1432)

On his part, Aquinas argues that "it is completely wrong to kill oneself....Hence for anyone to kill himself is to go against natural inclination and that charity whereby everyone is bound to love himself" (93). The Igbo believe that such an action attracts divine displeasure and brands it *Onwu Ojoo* ("Evil death").

Leonard points out that an act of suicide among the Igbo is looked on with manifest depreciation and horror: "It is generally spoken of as devilish or evil death" (260-261).

Suicide, on the account of its gravity is moral disorder, an attack on human life and on the lineage. As Amadi points out, in many parts of Igboland, there is a traditional practice of refusing worthy burial to one who commits suicide (76). The bodies of such people are disposed of in "Ajo Ohia" (Evil Forest). This fact is also dramatized more vividly by Achebe in *Things Fall Apart*, where Okonkwo's personal tragedy of suicide was shown and his being interred like 'a dog'. A passage in the book reads: "It is an offence against the earth, and a man who commits it will not be buried by his clansmen. His body is evil, and only strangers may touch it..." (146). The reason for this aversion to suicide seems to be that the Igbo see in it not only the violent termination of precious life which in turn desecrates "*Ala*" (Earth) but also ingratitude to the ancestors and community for their endowment to the deceased for a lifetime.

(iii) Abortion - Haring looks on abortion as "the deliberate ejection of the fruit of the womb from the mother's body or killing it while it is still in the womb. (276). Thiroux, on his part, describes abortion as the premature termination of a pregnancy prior to birth (210). Abortion seemed rare in Igbo pre-colonial epoch. What was common, according to Esomonu, was "miscarriage" (199). We speak of miscarriage as Pazhaym-Pallil posits, if pregnancy has been interrupted by causes which are beyond the control of the free will, such as infection,

trauma, incompetent cervix, illness of the mother and insufficient hormones. "Miscarriage" was regarded by the majority of people as loss of a human being. Generally, traditional morality militated against the easy attitude towards self-induced or deliberate abortion. Moreover, wilful abortion, like murder, was regarded by the people as "*Aru*" (abomination) which, as Arinze puts it, "embraces serious personal and moral crimes according to Igbo morality…such as patricide, suicide, incest and wilful abortion" (34).

However, we do not rule out completely or absolutely the possibility of wilful abortion in certain conflict situations. For instance, a couple involved with unwanted pregnancy, to avoid public ridicule and shame may decide to terminate such a pregnancy. The most common methods are the application of native concoctions and herbs supplied by medicine men (199). In such a situation, as "*Omenala*" (custom) demands, the couple may offer a sacrifice of purification to cleanse the land thus polluted. This is called "*Ikpu Ala,*" an elaborate sacrificial ritual. Through this mechanism, the Igbo emphasize and keep alive the active sense of the value of life and act in defence of the weakest and most innocent in the society.

Other deeds that attract serious punishments include incest, adultery, and stealing. Their punishments range from banishment from the clan, expiation through animal sacrifices, public/open exposure at the market square, payment of fines and confiscation of property for stealing.

Igbo Moral Philosophy

Igbo morality is distinctly communalistic. There exists the notion of corporate responsibility among the people. Whenever the well-being of the community is threatened through a violation of *ala* (the moral code), there is always a communal approach to the restoration of the ontological equilibrium. This morality scores several points over the extreme individualism sponsored by some Western philosophers whose moral philosophy, in many quarters, concentrate on the actions of the individuals without sufficient attention to the value-systems, norms and aspirations of society. However, "not only should the intentions of the individual but also the result of the collective action be looked for in judging the good" (Okere 13). For the Igbo with whom solidarity is truly significant, there is need for an elaborate ethic of the group. The ethic of the group assumes the first step towards the relativization of ethics itself.

From a secularist perspective, human law cuts lose from morality, and a distinction is made between crime and sin. In Igbo traditional society, this is not the case. Although, *Omenala* (the moral code) is not written as in the case of positive law, crimes are not transgressions of the "law" but factual contradictions of established order. It must be noted that the introduction of English criminal law proved quite perplexing to the Igbo mind. That a man known to be a murderer should be pronounced "Not guilty" and set free because of insufficient evidence or some other technicality was the height of absurdity. Depicting a reformatory, humanistic philosophy of punishment, Thomas Osborne who professed his avowed opposition to capital punishment argues that society must not brand a man a criminal, "but aim solely to reform the mental conditions under which a criminal act has been committed" (252). Such an argument against capital punishment might show more regard for the criminal than the victim of the crime. This weakens justice and encourages murder. It is based on a philosophical system that makes fetish of the idea that taking life is wrong under every circumstance. Moreover, the reformationist/ rehabilitationist penal theorists seem to undermine the fact that punishing crime in human society emanated more from the collective desire and will to preserve life and existence than from sheer love of punishing the criminal. Deterrence as an element of penal philosophy has never been an end in itself but a means of keeping within manageable proportions the common inclination in humans to be calculatingly aberrant especially when they consider the punishment to be light. While conceding that capital punishment may not always have a successful deterrent effect in all cases, it must be borne in mind that crime is the compulsive inclination of a depraved human nature. Hence, no humanistic philosophy of punishment may produce any meaningful reformation.

On the other hand, Igbo traditional morality with its strong emphasis on dos and do nots has a deontological character and is connected with the unchangeability of the code. The moral code (*Omenala*) is believed to have been handed down from time immemorial, and subsists as part of the natural order of things such as sunrise and sunset. Because of this rigidity, it developed a casuistry to inflict all sorts of severe punishment on culprits. One curious fact about crime and punishment in Igbo traditional society was that criminal motives were frequently not examined carefully, so that accidents were punished, as if they were deliberate crimes.

Traditional vs Western Penal Systems

That criminals and murderers are not only allowed to keep their lives but are met with more respect and care is absurd in African tradition and culture. This development that comes as part of Western "civilization" is contradictory to traditional morality that espouses both retributive and deterrent forms of justice. The situation in Europe today could somewhat be described as a growing reformationist approach to criminal justice. When we focus on the perpetrators of crimes, we see that this trend only leads to a romaticization of criminal tendencies and a degrading of the value placed on life (of the victims). The Igbo concept of crime and punishment partakes of a static principle, combining traditional heritage and the accrual of past forms and a dynamic principle through which morality remains always in crisis, always alive to contingency and growth. However inflexible and uncritical traditional morality may appear to the contemporary analytical mind, they helped pre-literate societies, like the Igbo, Yoruba and Hausa to cope with problems of their social existence and promote good and harmonious relations between individuals in society.

In this circumstance, a truly African philosophy must ensure that the traditional ideals of criminal justice are not relegated behind the criminal theories of the West. Violent criminals should instead be met with the right indignation that manifests in punishment in due proportion for their crimes. To believe that imprisonment would hold the chance of rehabilitation for gleeful and unrepentant murderers, instead of capital punishment, would be fatuous. Yet, the foregoing notwithstanding, crude methods of criminal adjudication and sentencing should not be retained in contemporary penal systems just because tradition demands so. While not throwing time-tested principles of morality and justice overboard, we can sift and adopt relevant penal systems as props to traditional morality. This creates room for complementarity of values and might truly be the right approach in our contemporary society.

Chapter 9

Naming in Esanland

EO Idiakheua and D Oamen

NAMING is universal human activity; its origin is as old as man. Science has attempted to give name to every breakthrough, hence we have the Archimedes' Principle, Hook's Law, Gay Lussack's Law, etc. Biologically, plants have their own (botanical) names and chemicals have their own (IUPAC) names. Also humans love their given names, nicknames, pennames and pseudonyms. Names are very important; they give identity and are evidence of recognition, and awareness of self.

In Africa, a name functions as a stamp of identity, an expression of belief, the feeling and understanding of a situation whether for a new born child or the one who has had a new born baby. Naming is consequently directed toward evoking a feeling or bringing about healing, succour, buffer, hope, and restoration to individuals thus helping them to cope with the situation at hand or in future. We will review a few names that serve for such coping among the Esan of Nigeria.

As useful as names serve in African societies, when associated with misfortune they generate tension, and the affected individual's self-image is tarnished. A named deemed repugnant may well up negative emotions like anger, hostility, aggression and distress. The affected people may therefore resort to changing their names. This review of Esan names reveals that a name is a reflection of self, current status, conditions and circumstances surrounding the events before or after birth, and within one's religious faith and place of birth. Such names are usually given by a father, grand father or head of the home. Thus Esan names reflect an individual's condition either in the past (*ariabhe*) or future (*ariana*). In Esanland a name clearly has psychological, cognitive and emotional functions. It serves as a source of hope, optimism and remembrance, and thus may bring about healing and restoration, enhancing the individual, the caller and the hearer. Consequently, the individual has good self esteem which in turn influences his perception and actions in society.

Psychology as a discipline concerned with human behaviour recognises that names assist the individuals to cope with emotions and dilemmas generated by human actions in life. Similarly, the Esan believe that the names given to children help them to cope better with problems that crop up in daily life. People whose state or condition may have led to some disqualification from being normal may be subjected to social isolation, stigmatization, scorn, pity, or psychological abuse. Thus the coping function of names needs to be understood as traditional psychotherapy and self help which heal the wounds incurred in daily living. A name also serves as a self-fulfilling prophesy. self-fulfilling prophecy, a concept developed by Robert K. Merton to explain how a belief or expectation, whether correct or not, affects the outcome of a situation or the way a person (or group) will behave.

..... Click the link for more information.Esan names have historic, political, poetic and managerial functions as coping elements. They appear in expressively great or exaggerated forms, sometimes with even political colouration. Such names include *Ineteabor,* meaning 'I am not in contest with them;' *Ibhadode* meaning 'I did not miss my way;' *Eloakale*, figuratively, 'you should eat one's appearance (look) before his food,' *Iyoodan*, meaning 'I am not a different person' and *Iriale,* meaning 'I will not mind.' It is in this regard that Omoregie classifies Edo names which include Esan names into nine areas they are ancient, dynasty, ancestral, deities, royal, colonial, modern, philosophical, idiomatic, and divine, while going on to signify that names in Africa, particularly in Esan land, are coping oriented (iii).

In 1969 Talbot observed what names stand for among the people of southern Nigeria where Esan belongs. In his view, in most tribes the child is given several names, the first usually that of the day on which it comes into the world, especially in the Central and Eastern regions, a second, alluding to the circumstances under which, it was born, whether at night, or in the bush, or whether the family is prosperous etc. Another is after a friend and a fourth that of the ancestors, or part of the over-soul, who is thought to be reincarnated in the babe (356). These views reveal the added value of African names. Igbe corroborates the above views and observations to a large extent. According to him:

the pomp and colour of a child naming event reflect a deep commitment to the child. The names they give are lessons in philosophy and their vision of life. The Edo do not threat a child's name as if it were a label. Rather than names of objects and places therefore, they give names that are brief statements about and prayers to the world, the home and environment. Sometimes they give names that mark the time, the event or the season in which the children were born. (53-54)

Igbe's view is more accurate being a practitioner and custodian of Edo naming culture of which Esan is a part. Talbot who must have sourced his information from a second party may not understand that the coping potency of Esan names or any other Edo names for that matter is built within the meaning of the name as shown in the above view. There is a need to understand the therapeutic function of names among the Esan people living in the southern part of Nigeria. Their dialect is a variety of the Edo and they share common language, religion, kingship, family and culture, though there is a little variation as one travels from one region to another. Their prominent occupation is farming, fishing and hunting as their land is thickly forested and blessed with a fertile climate with a part of the eastern boundary occupied by the River Niger. It is easily assessable as it forms the gateway to the northern part of Nigeria, from both the Niger Delta and the South East region.

Esan people are predominantly Christians, Muslims and African traditionalists. They are easily noted in the Catholic, Anglican and Pentecostals churches. Those who practise African Traditional Religion consult the local practitioners particularly when they have problems finding a solution to their problems. With a hereditary traditional kingship ruling system under the *Enogie* (traditional ruler) where the first male born child succeeds the father, there are several of these *Enogie* in the various kingdoms of Esan land. The average Esan child bears basically two names: an Esan name and a Christian name, though some are English names due to the influence of Christianity. A majority love to be called by their English names which to some degree are reactions to their privileged backgrounds, or they indicate an interest or admiration for the forerunner for whom they were named. These are usually popular, palatable, or comforting names which therefore supports the thesis that Esan names generally serve a psychological function. In this review we present the art of naming as a coping strategy among the Esan by listing the names that serve as a means of coping with such challenges of contemporary existence.

Esan names are characterized by time, events and situations. They are a reflection of Esan culture and way of life. To understand a name is therefore to understand the individual. They are also a means of communication. For instance, the name *Owobu* has the biological significance of a child that is born with the placenta round his neck. *Akomu* and *Anegbemu* mean if we cooperate the task of life will be easier, signifying the fact that we are born into a social network which sustains and gives us support in life. Ameikpoya *means* water can't cleanse the suffering or tears of life. *Ehikioya* and *Osekioya* mean it is God that wipes one's shame. Thus the name if for healing, cleansing, and for bringing pacification to the called, the caller and hearer.

Some names in Esanland are tended towards children, as they are the future of the family, community and nation. It is worthy to note that African life focuses on children. This can be seen in the type of names being given among the Esan. One frequently comes across names beginning with *Omon* meaning child. For example *Omoaka* means the children that we count, *Omogenfe:* child hails wealth; *Omoaghe:* we are looking at children, and *Omogbohu:* a child softens anger.

Valfre defines coping as any thought or action aimed at reducing stress and observes that we all use coping mechanism as tools that help us work through the ups and downs of daily living. She divides the coping mechanism into three main types, namely, psychomotor [physical] cognitive [intellectual] and affective [emotional] (19). A look at the names given to these people might reveal how it satisfies the emotional and cognitive functions of coping.

Most names in Esan satisfy coping criteria; they are means of releasing emotions or catharsis. They also serve other purposes as anger management, for example, *Omogbohu,* which means 'a child quells anger.' This name is used in settling a crisis, mostly hassles and face-offs, between husbands and wives.

It is worthy to remember that the presence of children also drives loneliness and ensures the continuation of life and the community. For example, *Omokhuabhie* and *Ekiomoado* mean 'we are in the business for children.' It is worthy to realise that children constitute the main reason for marriage among Africans which reinforces their companionship and support roles in the extended and multigenerational family.

Aremoineme; ireho nebho is a name that states when you conceal a matter from me I will void hearing it. This is a consolatory name: We are concerned with what we hear; what we do not know we are not worried about it. These names help in reducing anxiety, so it also releases pent-up tension resulting from everyday encounters.

The arrival of new baby is a period of rejoicing and names that symbolises release of tension are given. Examples of such names are *Oiloghose*, meaning it is not difficult for God; *Iwenoise:* work of God or handwork of God resulting probably from the built up tension of public expectancy; *Akhamiojie,* meaning when you see a king you stammer and all your boasts come to an end. The same goes for *Aitaegbebhunu* meaning we do not talk on each other's presence. This is a revelation about human nature, where few would speak the truth in your presence.

Abhameso means they have added lies to my words. This name is significant as no two people will present same matter in same way. The name releases pent up feelings on the part of the bearer. Esan names are often a subjective interpretation of situations and give insight into future expectations. For instance, believing in God for a child, mostly when he had suffered secondary infertility, the Esan man may exercise his faith thus: *Oriabure*, meaning it is for someone that you join (in marriage); *Otuokpaikhian,* meaning one cannot go on alone, which is a major belief among men that it is not good to live alone without a help mate. *Imoibighe* means I have something I am looking at. This means that there are latent (hidden) features in humans, so everyone admires one another for different reasons.

Ebaide means what you can't buy. This name is used to buttress the belief that children are not what you can purchase at a displayed price and specification. Esan names are also given when a specific sex dominates in a family, e.g., females. The names are used to indicate mastery of life situations e.g. *Aiguiyen,* and *Ojiagbonaye* mean no one lives without making mistakes, and we are in a world full of wonders. *Elolen* means eyes can see human secrets even if the mouth does not talk. The meaning as given above brings a sense of relief to the individual who tells his/ her perceived enemies: 'I see what you are doing even if I do not talk about it.'

Whether from religious faith or natural human tendency for great expectations, Esan names generally strive to radiate hope. *Ederibhalo* and *Edewede* mean there is hope when there is more time. *Edewede:* the day is yet to come. These names reflect hope in the community. Names like *Oziengbe*, (male) *Iziengbe*, (female) are declarations that who have endured will rejoice, and that patience is golden. *Ebegbezien* refers to what the individual has endured or persevered.

Oseghale literally means God is the one that endows, so I should not be envied. This name is usually given to males who perpetuate the family lineage. Survival and propagation is a basic need for every man. So the birth of a male child is received with gladness as the male children help in retaining the family name. Sometimes a name such as *Ibhadode, Ibhadojemu* or *Imadojemu* is given as a declaration: I did not buy it; I did not steal it, as it is God-given. To justify the belief that it is God that gives children and wealth the Esan man gives names like *Ebehiriere,* meaning what God gave. *Ehiremen, Oseremen, Oseriere, Osagie and Ehigie*, all mean 'God gives' or 'God sent.'

Airoboze (You do not choose) signifies that a lifestyle, or giving birth to a particular sex, is not by choice. *Airudubie* and *Airohubie* argue that you do not give birth by your power, or by your anger. Esan names indicate that life belongs to God and that the ability to give birth is not by human power but God's. The Esan place high hopes in their deity.

Okhuoiyoshoman means woman is not our friend echoing the paternalistic and male chauvinist slogan: "a beautiful woman never stays with one man."

Onobhamionriobe asserts that who has not seen a bad person knows how to live well. This goes to mean if you have a bad woman life becomes difficult, as everybody hears and knows your life in the community.

A corollary to the above would include names like *Oribhunuebho, Ebhodaghe* and *Eleobhosebho,* meaning your lifestyle is under watch as people see and witness what you do. *Omonzele* means a child is a strong reason for our behaviour as they are the propagators of the family and the future of humanity. This name may also come as *Ebhozele*, meaning people are the cause of our actions. The moral is that no man is an island unto himself. He lives in a community and is part of a network of social beings.

Agboinzebeta is a name that says: do not bother about what people say. This name has a salutary effect on both rich and poor: when two people are seated it is a natural thing among them to discuss others as they attempt to explain what is going on in other people's lives. In response to this a wealthy family may give their child the name *Ekeonomoifu,* meaning those who have wealth are always envied. It is worthy to note that the rich may resort to names like *Egbomeade,* meaning 'they are threatening me.' Another name of value is *Elenbesunu* or sometimes *Alenbesunu,* meaning 'they know what has happened' or 'they are asking questions' or 'we should know what happened.'

Aidoyen means you do not or cannot live in secret, as people are seeing you. This adage is also reflected in names such as *Ojemoeva* and *Aituajie* which aver that laughter has two types - one may be to laugh at the victim, while the other is to rejoice, so you don't rush into laughing at somebody, as nobody knows tomorrow.

Isimemen means where I am (probably a strange land) is good for me. *Enosekhale*: whatever God prepares must come to pass; *Agbonyanegbe:* it is the world that hates and discriminates and these can result to other things like stereotyping and killing. In Esan *Aimiemibhobe* means no gain in evil, so let's put it all to a stop. *Obemeata* and *Aitebiremen* seem a lamentation: they talk of my evil deeds; they do not talk of my good. *Ekata* and *Ekaniyere*: how many can I say; I can only say the number I remember.

Osedebamen asserts that God is with me, so I will not weary, faint or die. Its biblical equivalent is Emmanuel, God with us. *Oseahumen* means God is my might. *Emibhanomionria* avers that nothing is greater than a brother. While *Onohuome, Enowosemeame, Aroboinosen* are declarations that who wishes good, gets good; who wishes mine to be good, his too will be good, and if we all do well, it will be well.

These names help in bringing relief to the caller, thus helping him to cope with daily life:

Ighoomoijalo: The money used in rearing on a child cannot be calculated.
Irumudomon: For the sake of children.
Eguakhide: This kingdom will not fall
Aimiejagbonse: There is no end to life
Aigbibhaluemi: You do not beat an innocent man
Aragbonfo: We have come to the world already so let them say what they like
Agbontalo: People are talking.
Obhafuoso: No one is free of problems or issues.

Ekemeilenlen: It is only my own mind that I know; I don't know the mind of others.
Aitenoria: You can't suffer another's disgrace.
Ibhaghewan: I was not sensible early enough.
Enimiehomon: The ones I see are children.
Enatomen: This is what I desired, i.e. which pains me most.
Iribhogbe: I am in my kingdom.
Ogbemudia: My kingdom has stood (firm).
Ahine: You came to this world with your destiny.
Aisagbonhi: You do not come to earth to plan your destiny.
Idialu: I will live to achieve success.
Ohuomoirie: You can't be annoyed with a child.

The use of names as a means of coping among Esan people fulfils the purpose of cognitive restructuring, problem solving and reality coping therapy which reflect on basic human tendencies toward maintaining and enhancing self-actualisation. Such is the forward movement of life where human behaviour is fundamentally a set of goal directed attempts by the organism to satisfy experienced needs. All needs can ultimately be subsumed under the single urge of enhancement of the phenomenal self. Alderian theorises that the general goal of life is to gain the mastery over the environment by coping with the task of work, belonging, and social interactions and so reality therapy maintains that people have the basic needs of love and belonging, followed by needs to gain self-worth, respect, and recognition (46). This provides for sound mental health which is manifested in ability to cope with daily stress.

It is worthy to know that the names given to children might serve as means to fulfil such goals in life. It also satisfies the tenets of cognitive therapies as elucidated by scholars like Paul Dubois, Alfred Adler, Albert Bandura, Albert Ellis and Joseph Cautella the main goal of which is to replace dysfunctional beliefs and thoughts in order to cause a change in personal view points.

Chapter 10

Rhythms: in Honour of Achebe

Emezue and Roy (Guest)

'Ekwefi and Ezinma still remain my favourite characters' –AG Roy

CE: Tell me more about the Mysore conference where you presented a paper on Achebe with a hundred and fifty students and faculty from various colleges in Karnataka participating.

AGR: The Mysore conference was an attempt by Mahadeva Kunderi, the present chair of the department of English in the university, to revive the department's glorious history. The department has had on its faculty some of the founding fathers of Commonwealth Literature, including CD Narasimhaiah, HH Anniah Gowda and others pioneering the teaching by organising several conferences on post-colonial literatures, including some on African literature in the 1980s. CD Narasimhaiah and Anniah Gowda were instrumental in introducing a course that included African writings in English in the University of Mysore and subsequently in other universities in the South. The department continued to flourish under the leadership of creative writers such as the noted Kannada novelist, UR Ananthamurthi, and other doyens of Commonwealth Literature: C P Belliappa, CP Ravichandra, and so on, until the late 1990s.

I have no hesitation in stating that the department more than lived up to its legendary academic reputation through the overwhelming participation of students and teachers of colleges and universities in the southern state of Karnataka. The best part of the Conference, in my view, were the reminiscences shared by senior Mysore academics who had the distinction of having interacted with Achebe during his visit to Mysore and the impact Achebe had on the then budding academics on writing, teaching, canon-formation and criticism. Many of them could quote Achebe verbatim and even recall his body language and mannerisms. It appeared fitting that academics who were inspired by the foremost literary legend should congregate after so many years to pay their respects to him on this solemn occasion.

CE: Well that's truly adorable.

Before your recent your entry 'Oral-Written Interface: The Folktale in Achebe's Fiction' which got you cited as Writer of the Year 2011, you had on record a work of great enthusiasm, 'Oral Rhythms of Achebe's Fiction' and I am wondering: Is African literature perceived in Indian circles mostly in context of Achebe's classics or just special interest you have in that unique talent from the continent?

AGR: 'Oral Rhythms of Achebe's Fiction' was one of my earliest publications. In fact, it formed a Chapter in my PhD dissertation "Oral Traditions in Three Nigerian Novelists: Achebe, Soyinka and Tutuola." Incidentally, my PhD dissertation in 1988 was one of the earliest doctoral theses submitted in an Indian institution at a time African literature was hardly known in Indian universities except in the south such as the University of Madras from where I obtained my Masters due to the initiatives of pioneers like Narasimhaiah. I am happy to note that most Indian universities include a paper or, at least, few texts on African literature in their curriculum now. Unfortunately, other than among serious students of literature, there is little awareness about African writers - like Achebe or anyone else for that matter. At my institution, however, we attempt to sensitize our students to contemporary concerns such as racial discrimination through teaching Soyinka's "Telephone Conversation." I must say I'm happy to note that some of them are sufficiently hooked to African writing once they have a context to move on to other African writers.

CE: I believe it would be fair to call you an important authority on Achebe today. How did this enterprise of specialty on 'beleaguered' African literature begin for you and who were your motivators in this area?

AGR: I am humbled and honoured to be considered an authority and feel I have made some contribution to

Achebe criticism when I see my earliest publications being cited in Wikipedia. I was attracted to Achebe's fiction after reading Things Fall Apart as part of an optional paper on Commonwealth Literature while a Masters student in Stella Maris College affiliated to the University of Madras. I would settle for nothing else as topic for my PhD after I discovered Achebe despite senior scholars' efforts to prevail upon me not to explore uncharted territories.

CE: No doubt Achebe will live forever in the memories of those who knew or talked with him in the commonwealth of world writing. I share the humour in his last interview that Things Fall Apart is even more popular than himself. Nadime Gordimer who called him the father of modern African literature recently idolised Achebe's uncommon boldness and courage in those years describing the novel as 'prescient' of the post colonial and later violence that was to descend on Africa's political and cultural landscape. Well, taking the totality of his art in consideration, I am curious to discover which Indian contemporary, along with Ananthamurthi already mentioned, comes closest to approximating the indigenous approach to literary heritage? Who would you recommend to an African scholar interested in engaging modern Indian fiction in relative parlance?

AGR: Although they started writing much earlier in the 1930s, but two Indian novelists -Raja Rao and RK Narayan- come closest to Achebe's indigenous approach to literary heritage in their liberal borrowings from indigenous narrative and aesthetic traditions. If Raja Rao's Kanthapura is structured like asthalapurana [legend of a place] narrated by the grandmother character in the manner Indian grandmothers narrate tales to young adults, his Serpent and the Rope is stylistically structured like philosophical Upanishad dialogues. On the other hand, the disarming simplicity with which RK Narayan reconstructs the life-rhythms of the fictional town of Malgudi is strongly reminiscent of Achebe's apparently simple narrative style. Like Achebe, these novelists invented a variety of English to capture the speech patterns of their native Kannada and Tamil respectively. However, their fiction, despite its nationalist underpinnings, is not overtly political as Achebe's writings. The novelist who described himself as a political writer, and who we claim as ours, is Salman Rushdie who borrows from both Hindu and Islamic heritage of the Panchtantra and Mahabharata as well as from the Indo-Islamic qissas and the dastans.

CE: That's quite interesting. Also looking from your study of Achebe, Soyinka and Tutuola, how might traditional Nigerian fiction and culture be seen to contrast with its Indian oral counterpart?

AGR: Indian oral traditions exhibit very strong convergences with (and divergences from) traditional Nigerian fiction and culture. When I read translations of Igbo and Yoruba genres compiled by folklorists, I was struck by the similarities between the content and form of Igbo and Yoruba folktales and Indian Panchtantra and

Jataka tales as well as between African and Indian creation myths. I must confess that I learnt to formally deconstruct Indian folk traditions through my readings in Igbo and Yoruba folklore. My research on African oral traditions inspired my book Bhangra Moves: From Ludhiana to London and Beyond (Aldershot: Ashgate 2010) on bhangra, a Punjabi performance genre that has become part of global popular culture and on other narrative and performing traditions such as the Persoarabic qissas, dastans and Bengali patachitras.

CE: Do you have other work on Achebe's latter novels such as Anthills of the Savannah or A Man of the People or are you mainly interested in those set within the pre-colonial periods like Things Fall Apart and Arrow of God?

AGR: Of course, I am as interested in his novels set in the postcolonial period as in those set in the pre-colonial. For one, there is a seamless glide from the pre-colonial to the post-colonial in the trilogy that foregrounds the continuity between the pre-colonial and postcolonial Nigerian condition. Besides Achebe's engagement with the form that the nation takes in Nigeria, the production of the national subject and the conflict between old tribal affiliations and new discourse of citizenship has a deep resonance with the situation in other traditional postcolonial societies, particularly India. While postcolonial disillusionment of A Man of the People reverberates with a similar disenchantment among intellectuals in post independent India, the dark overtones of Anthills of the Savannah carry disquieting messages for other 'deviant' nationalisms in other postcolonial democracies.

CE: I am somewhat wondering why you didn't join the feminist wagon of literary appreciation, the type that fascinates gender stalwarts intent on reading phallocentric subjectivities in the works and criticisms of 'the early moderns' as we had termed them. Do you think all that western feminist posture against both writers was a valid approach to understanding Achebe's and Soyinka's cultural and artistic vision of the twentieth century?

AGR: I began my research when feminism had just become a fashionable word in India and most of my contemporaries have either made outstanding significant contributions to the feminist movement or to feminist criticism. My problem with my activist friends and feminist scholars was that euro-american feminist theory failed to account for alternative feminisms – African-American womanism or more subtle forms of resistance that accord women in traditional patriarchal societies. However, I do appreciate the light that western and postcolonial feminist scholars have thrown on Achebe's and Soyinka's aesthetic and cultural blueprint for the 20th century and the novelists' incorporation of that criticism in the construction of female subjectivities in their latter novels such as 'Anthills.' But Ekwefi and Ezinma still remain my favourite characters as their gentle strength reminds me of similar characters in Indian fiction and society.

CE: I can agree that true strength is, indeed, gentle.

Notwithstanding their enthusiasm for Achebe and Soyinka, a few young Indian scholars I have met seem to shy from such higher aesthetic concerns you delineate, preferring Emecheta's gender conflict. In fact, all they're able to write about is Emecheta, tradition and subjection of womanhood. I am thinking this might have more to do with society and its dualistic measure of women as symbols of mythological veneration and, as yet, objects of cultural subjection.

AGR: A number of Indian scholars, beginning in the late 1980s, were deeply engaged with gender issues particularly during the feminist wave that swept India around that period. I have been extremely impressed by the sophisticated analyses done by some of these scholars on African or Indian women writers borrowing feminist theories but a large part of the criticism appears to be thematic analyses of women's issues as represented in women's fiction. I would have been happy to see in feminist literary analysis a sustained engagement with the dichotomy between the symbolic veneration of women through goddess cults and the largely patriarchal framework within which women still continue to operate in traditional societies. I was particularly struck by the resemblance between the earth goddess, Ala, in Achebe's fiction and Mammy Wata, in Soyinka's works, and the goddess cults in India. But, as you have mentioned, they reproduce patriarchal veneration of female characters as goddess figures even as women continue to be oppressed in their real lives. I was extremely intrigued by Taila's character in Soyinka's Season of Anomy but it seemed to work, like that of his other female characters, at the symbolic rather than narrative level.

CE: With national literatures moving into their own identities and individual aesthetic preoccupations, hasn't the idea of literature of the commonwealth stymied as obsolete discourse? Surely, Achebe and scholars must have foreseen this inevitable course with his historic tour de force against imperial critical standards that Europe had attempted to graft upon the conquered territories in their time.

AGR: I began my research when the writings I worked on were classified as Commonwealth writing and I found myself floundering when I resumed active research after a seven-year hiatus. I found myself floundering in the new discipline of postcolonial theory. Not only had Commonwealth become an obsolete category for examining national literatures but also appeared theoretically naïve compared to the complex postcolonial discourse that had emerged with the publication of the essays of Bhabha, Spivak and others. I would strongly agree that Achebe and scholars had foreseen this inevitable course through their resistance to colonial discourse but I would not hesitate to state that their writings also interrogate the discursive indenturement of metropolitan postcolonial discourse to the west.

CE: At present, how has the decline in Ghandhi's spiritual legacy affected Indian political, cultural, attitudinal and corporate national outlook?

AGR: Gandhian spiritual legacy lives on quietly in a handful of intellectuals, political and spiritual leaders but the larger body of the nation appears to be completely taken over by the capitalist, corporate dream of consumerist cornucopia that sits at odd with the aesthetic of abstinence that Gandhi propagated and several generations of Indians embodied in their own life-styles. 'I buy therefore I am' appears to be 21st century India's new mantra that percolates to the level of the working classes whose aspirations are predictably coloured by the consumer goods they are surrounded with! To me there appears to be a complete ideological shift in India that is visible not only at the political but also cultural and attitudinal levels despite tokenist Gandhian gestures made by the state and certain individuals.

CE: Would you analyse the historical violence of India and Pakistan -not forgetting India's internal religious crises- along with the trend in Islamic terrorism that is currently ravaging northern Nigerian and West African nations, just like Achebe had predicted with his work, as the collision of worlds in a vicious cycle of brutality?

AGR: Certainly!
Historical violence of India and Pakistan, and India's looming internal religious crisis -partition 1947, anti-Sikh riots of 1984, Bombay bombings, Godhra - are really the

collision of worlds in a vicious cycle of brutality. Indian scholars have been grappling with violence of partition even seven decades after the event and have yet to explain it. The roots of internecine war or pathological violence, as communal violence is often described by historians and social theorists, would appear to lie deep in epistemic violence that comes with the displacement of traditional feudal societies with modern secular democratic formations.

CE: How can we hold a personal optimistic vision of this cycle that engulfs our destiny or would you subscribe to scholarly tendencies that dissect only theories from the practice of collective social reengineering?

AGR: As a third generation descendant of families who fled ethnic violence during partition 1947, the event is far removed from the post memories of my parents' generation whose lives were directly impacted by the event of partition. But I should not be able to dissect only theories from the practice of collective social reengineering.

CE: So what do you see as your personal philosophy of life, your vision of the world, its future? Could literature live up to that optimism of social and cultural transformation of our environment in more practical ways and purposes than have been envisioned of it?

AGR: My vision of the world is very Utopian. I dream of a world in which everyone would have clean air, water and food and there would be no suffering.

Literature, in my opinion, can definitely bring about social and cultural transformation. One only needs to think of the role played by writers like Rabindranath Tagore, and Bankim Chandra Chatterjee, Munshi Premchandin and the nationalist movement in the Indian context or of Wole Soyinka, Ngugi wa Thiong'o, Chinua Achebe or Christopher Okigbo in the African. However, one cannot forget that literature does not always directly work towards ushering in social and cultural transformation but proceeds in a more subtle manner.

CE: Agreeably, as our quantum universe proves, the passionate intensities of engagements are ultimately reducible to the most subtle dynamics.

Now what's your take on the unconscionable poverty and environmental degradation in India and the Third World in spite of some vaunted economic and technological achievements on the official table?

AGR: I don't think about it because it makes me impossibly sad. When I compare people in my country scrounging for essentials that people throw way without a second thought in the developed world, I wonder if there was a more equitable way of sharing the earth's resources. The ecologic crisis appears to be a luxury people obsessed with consumption do not appear to have time for.

CE: With Third World institutions falling all over like a pack of cards what is your Indian experience in the collapsing standard of education and scholarship that bedevils far too deeply the economy of developing nations?

AGR: I cannot complain as I have the privilege of teaching in one of the best institutions in India, namely the Indian Institute of Technology (IIT), which admits students through one of the most competitive examinations in the world. The joke is that IIT applicants keep MIT as a backup these days. However, I have noticed a sharp decline in real learning of the students I have taught for two and a half decades due to the overpowering instrumental orientation that drives young people in developing nations in the global era. The Humanities have tended to suffer in developing nations as they cannot sustain the creative economy. As a consequence, the best students in India gravitate towards the sciences, engineering, medicine, management, and so on, rather than literature or the arts.

CE: Let's go back to what you said somewhere that 'African preference for Bollywood melodrama to Hollywood finesse is a form of resistance to the western narratives of modernity.' [The Journal of African Literature and Culture No. 7, 2010] Given the sham that 'Bolly,' 'Nolly' and, indeed, all the 'Woods' represent to authentic cultural expressions, I do not truly believe the choice of melodrama over artistic restraint and discipline holds much promise for Asiatic and African cultures in a post modern world.

AGR: If you were to look at the box office collections of the 'Woods' in their domestic markets and the dent, however minor, Bollywood has made overseas, melodrama certainly appear to hold much promise for Asiatic and African cultures in a postmodern world. You may love Bollywood or hate Bollywood in India but you cannot escape it. It is here, there, everywhere. Melodrama offers a catharsis for collective emotion that artistic restraint and discipline fails to produce, at least among the masses, in the developing world.

CE: As you averred, the idea of India that appears to have inspired a variety of activities in Africa had ranged from Indian political movements on African resistance struggles and the conflict between communal value systems and modernity. Yet both societies were largely unsuccessful in stemming the wave of westernisation and the danger it posed to indigenous cultures and ways of life? Why did they seem to fail in warding off the west where China and Japan fairly succeeded to a comparative extent?

AGR: I think India has found a way of reconciling westernisation with tradition since the colonial era through the appropriation of the binary division of the public and the private in western modernity as the spaces of western modernity and tradition respectively. Indigenous Indian cultures and ways of life are still alive and kicking even though they have been transformed through their contact with modernity. Hereditary painters in a village in West Bengal now connect with prospective buyers through cell phones; they paint pictures of contemporary events such as the tsunami and 9/11 using traditional mythical frameworks, and hereditary musicians compose songs on 'the divine call' that is communicated through the telephone!

CE: Well that's intriguing.

Today, given the exploits of Bollywood and its newfangled fixation for western capitalism and elite values, wouldn't it be sanguine to note that Asia and Africa must not remain the economic and cultural prey of Europe in the asphyxiation of their ancient religious and philosophical traditions?

AGR: The current Bollywood fad for yoga, bhangra and 'Bollywood in the West' appears to me to be a form of neo-orientalism that preys on non-western artistic production for its own ends. The systematic destruction of indigenous knowledge systems by colonialism is a story that needs to be written again and again. However, as I mentioned, these systems are too resilient to be decimated and I find it extremely heartening to see youth in India embrace them as alternative lifestyles.

CE: Finally, a little about you: who is Anjali Gera Roy and what other interests engage her company apart from teaching African literature in English?

AGR: I would describe myself as an average academic who has reached the peak of her mediocrity but who gets a particular kick out of reading obscure critical and literary texts. I am a failed creative writer who puts on creative airs.

CE: What language is your mother tongue? What does 'Anjali' and 'Gera' mean from your indigenous semantic?

AGR: My mother tongue is Punjabi that I speak haltingly due to my grandparents' forced migration to another ethno linguistic region in India from West Punjab (present day Pakistan) to another ethno linguistic region in India after partition in 1947. In fact, they spoke a language that has now been renamed Siraiki and become the fulcrum of a separatist ethno linguistic movement in Pakistan. The word Anjali literally means a 'cupped palm' in Hindi and, metaphorically, it means the offerings of flowers or anything else that are made to the deities during Hindu prayers. Gera is a sub-caste of the Arora caste in Punjab who can be both Hindu and Sikh and traditionally engaged in trade.

CE: African communities are equally bogged by issues of tribal and clannish ethnicities. So the caste is still powerful a system of self and group identification in today's India as it appeared in times past.

AGR: Raised in a progressive Arya Samaji Hindu home, I was innocent of the meaning of caste until reaching adulthood when I came into contact with others for whom caste was a reality. Although caste origins are immaterial to modern, educated urban Indians, rural India is still split along ethnic and caste lines and ethnicity and caste are often key factors in electoral politics.

CE: Yeah. Sounds like Africa.
What other languages do you speak?

AGR: In addition to Hindi, English and Punjabi, I speak Bengali, the language spoken in West Bengal, where I have been living for almost a quarter of a century.

CE: Indians like their African brothers and sisters are now a mix-mash of identities. On a lighter note, would you call yourself an Indian traditionalist, a modern or New Age amalgam of the bhakti devotee and born again Christian believer?

AGR: I see myself as a modern Indian with Punjabi Hindu origins.

CE: So your religion is still the Hindu faith? Is there such a thing as modern or reformed Hindu as against the ancient Hindu practice we know?

AGR: There are many ways of practising Hinduism within India and there have been several movements within Hinduism over the centuries that have interrogated established religion and practices. Arya Samaj was a relatively new reform movement emerging at the end of the 19th century that attempted to simplify established Hindu rituals by returning to ancient Vedic texts and practices. I am afraid I am not a practicing Hindu but follow Hindu practices whenever the occasion arises.

CE: What are your hobbies, Anjali? And who have been your greatest motivators in your academic and other life pursuits?

AGR: Not too many. I use creative writing or cooking as stress-busters. I have been motivated by my former teachers, some from high school and others from the university, in my academic pursuits. My supervisor Viney Kirpal has been a role model of sorts but I am not able to keep up with her. In my other pursuits, of course, I think I am still trying to catch up with my homemaker mother who was not allowed to pursue a career due to the patriarchal world she grew up in despite being many times more talented than I could ever be.

CE: What favourite creative medium do you use to bust stress? Poetry? Prose?

AGR: Prose. Short stories that I would have long consigned to the rubbish bin but for active encouragement from writer friends.

CE: I should think your creative expression as remarkable as your scholarly enterprise. Are you not considering a publishing project for your creative work for the inspiration of, importantly, the Anjali Gera Roy posterity?

AGR: You must be joking! A few odd pieces of creative writing in a journal with limited circulation does not make one a writer! If I could find a way of doing it, I would like to write a novel about the Indian Partition of 1947.

CE: Where is Viney Kirpal now? Are you working closely with her as you did in the beginning of your academic career?

AGR: Viney Kirpal took premature retirement at the peak of her academic career and started a second career as a corporate trainer and consultant. She now runs an NGO that trains school and college teachers and has won the highest accolades for the work she has been doing. I continue to contribute to the many books on pedagogy that she has edited in the last two decades but have not been able to persuade her to return to literary pursuits.

CE: You must have this sense of connection to Africa like many intellectuals who have held some measure of fascination for the continent as reflected by their life's works.

AGR: Yes, I do. I am more fascinated by the links between India and Africa in the past than in the present. I have been following the journeys of Sikhs to Africa in the late nineteenth century and of African travellers to India earlier.

CE: What comes out as most likeable or worthy of public note in your discoveries around African and Sikh interactions in the early days? It was rather unfortunate that peaceable relations could not persevere and, with the partition that was rather mired in the spates of violence that began at the turn of the nineteenth century, the endearing legacies of Indus Valley civilisation to the world have been consequently short changed.

AGR: The friendship was between Sikh pioneers like Kala Singh and the East African people. I would like to know more about Sikh-African relations but have found nothing more than anecdotal evidence about the mixing between Sikhs and their African hosts. It is interesting that 'twice migrant Sikhs' in the UK, US and Canada have very fond memories of Africa despite their eviction and look upon Africa rather than Punjab as home.

CE: Surely one of these days your connection to Africa must be strong enough to bring you to Africa on some kind of kindred spirit connection ...

AGR: I was invited to speak at a Wole Soyinka Conference in Nigeria the occasion of Soyinka's 80th birthday but could not make it due to a number of reasons. If I had been able it would have been a dream come true.

CE: Anjali let me thank you for coming and contributing your talent to our efforts. As a distant admirer of your good self since the eighties, I am proud to see you here as one of our millennial Writers of the Year!

AGR: I am pleasantly surprised and happy that you and others in parts of the African world were reading my essays in the eighties. Acceptance of my work by African scholars is the only reward I seek for the little contribution I have made to the field and makes the intellectual journey I made then well worth the effort.

END

Notes and Bibliography

Chapter 1
African Storytelling and Development

Works Cited

Apronti, E. O. "The Writer in Our Society." *Literature and Modern West African Culture.* Ed. D. I. Nwoga. Benin City: Ethiope Publishing, 1978.

Chinweizu, Ihechukwu Madubuike, Onwuchekwa Jemie. *Toward the Decolonisation of African Literature.* Enugu: Fourth Dimension, 1980.

Aig-Imoukhuede, F. (ed.) *A Hand Book of Nigeria Culture.* Lagos: Department of Culture, 1991.

Emezue, GMT. "Literature and Conflict Resolution in Africa: Discussions with Seven Nigerian Authors." Ed. Charles Smith. *Journal of African Literature* 5, 2008 (339-359).

Egudu, R. N. "Igbo Traditional Poetry and Family Relationship." *Literature and Modern West African Culture.* D. I. Nwoga. Benin City: Ethiope Publishing, 1978.

Nkatia, J.H.K. *Safeguarding Traditional Culture and Folklore in Africa.* Accra, Ghana: International Centre for Africa Music and Dance, 1999.

Rohmer, M. "Patterns of Communication: Wole Soyinka's Death and the King's Horseman and Royal Exchange Theatre Production, Manchester." Ed. Eckhard Brectinger. *Theatre and Performance in Africa.* Bayreuth: African Series, 2003.

Oamen, Osedebamen. "Storytelling as a Contributory Factor to the Discrimination against Women." *Multidisciplinary Journal of Research Development,* vol. 9, 2007. 128.

Rodney, Water. *How Europe Underdeveloped Africa.* Abuja: Panaf, 1972.

Chapter 2
Female Bonding in Black Literature

Works Cited

Branzburg, Judith V. "Seven Women and a Wall." *Callaloo* 21 (1984): 116-119.

Christian, Barbara. *Black Women Novelists: The Development of a Tradition, 1892-1976.* Connecticut: Greenwood Press, 1980.

Dill, Bonnie Thornton. "Race, Class, and Gender: Prospects for an All-inclusive Sisterhood." *Feminist Studies* 9.1 (1983): 131-150.

Fowler C. Virginia. *Gloria Naylor: In Search of Sanctuary.* New York: Twayne Publishers, 1996.

Harris, Trudier. "This Disease Called Strength: Some Observation on the Compensating Construction of Black Female Character". *Literature and Medicine* 14.1 (1995): 109- 126.

Henderson, Carol E. "Freedom to Self-create: Identity and the Politics of Movement in Contemporary African American Fiction." *Modern Fiction Studies* 46. 4 (2000): 998-1003.

Hooks, Bell. *Feminist Theory: from Margin to Center.* Boston: South End Press, 1984.

Hooks, Bell. "Sisterhood: Political Solidarity between Women." *Feminist Review* 23 (1986): 125-138.

Hooks, Bell and McKinnon, Tanya. "Sisterhood: Beyond Public and Private". *Signs* 21. 4 (1996): 814-829.

Jewell, K. Sue. *From Mammy to Miss America and Beyond: Cultural Images and the Shaping of US Social Policy.* New York: Routledge, 1993.

Khay, Renee. "The Ties that Bind: Female Relationships in the Works of Gloria Naylor." *Associatedocument.com* (Web). 6 December 2006.

Kulkarni, Harihar. *Black Feminist Fiction: A March Towards Liberation.* New Delhi: Creative Books, 1999.

Matus, Jill J. "Dream, Deferral, and Closure in *The Women of Brewster Place*". *Black American Literature Forum* 24.1 (1990): 49-64.

Montgomery, Maxine Lavon. *The Apocalypse in African-American Fiction.* University Gainesville: Press of Florida, 1996.

Naylor, Gloria. *The Women of Brewster Place.* London and Sydney: Sphere Books Limited, 1984.

Naylor, Gloria. *Mama Day.* New York: Ticknor & Fields, 1988.

Smith, Valerie, et al (ed). *African American Writers' Profile of Their Lives and Works—From the 1700s to the Present.* New York: MacMillan Publishing Co, 1993.

Webb, Claudia Lawrence et al. "African American Intergender Relationships: A Theoretical Exploration of Roles of Patriarchy, and Love." *Journal of Black Studies* 34.5 (2004): 623-639.

Whitt, Margaret Earley. *Understanding Gloria Naylor.* Columbia: University of South Carolina Press, 1999.

Chapter 3
Insigamigani (Heroic) Traditions

Works Cited

Benedigito Mulihano, *Ibirari By'insigamigani*, Kigali, Imprimerie Nationale, 2005.

Bussman H., *Routledge Dictionary of Language.* London: Routledge, 1996.

Dagger, Richard, Rights, Boundaries, and the Bonds of Community: A Qualified Defense of Moral Parochialism, American Political Science Review, 1985, 79: 436-47.

Drisko G. "A Blueprint for Democratic Citizenship Education in South Africa." *South African Journal of Education.* 1993. EASA Vol.26 (1)129-142.

Hawthorne Jeremy, *A Glossary of contemporary literary theory,* New York, Routledge, 1994.
Miller, Richard. "Killing for the Homeland: Patriotism, Nationalism and Violence." The Journal of Ethics. Vol. 1, No. 2. Springer, Web. 11.2011 www.jstor.org/stable/25115543
Mukarutabana, Rose-Marie. *Gakondo: The Oral Literature of Rwanda.* Web. 11.2011 www.webspinners.com
Northrop Frye, *Anatomy of Criticism.* Princeton: Princeton University Press, 1947.
Primoratz, Igor, and Pavković, Aleksandar (eds.) *Patriotism: Philosophical and Political Perspectives*, Aldershot: Ashgate Publishing, 2008.
Propp Vladimir, *Morphology of the Folktale.* Austin: University of Texas Press, 1970.
Rutayisire Paul et.al. Incamake y'amateka y'u Rwanda kuva mu Ntangiriro kugeza mu mpera y'ikinyejana cya 20, Rwanda National Reconciliation Commission, 2010.
Smirnov, Oleg. *Ancestral War and the Evolutionary Origins of Heroism.* Oregon: Stony Brook University, 2007.

Chapter 4
Rumuji Women's Dance

Works Cited
Chisa Abel. Oral interview. Emohua Town, May 2010. Np.
Enekwe, O. *Theories of Dance in Nigeria.* Nsukka: Afa Press, 1991.
Habermans et al. *ABC of Dialectical and Historical Materialism.* Moscow: Progress Publishers, 1979.
Jane, Parpart. 'Women and the State in Africa.' *The Precarious Balance, State and Society in Africa.* Eds. Rothchild and Chazen. Boulder: Westview, 1988.

Krama, I.C. *African Traditional Theatre and Drama*: Themes and Perspectives. Choba: Akpokem International, 2006.

Nyeche, Chief. Oral interview. Rumuji. Rivers State, May 2010. Np.

Peil, Margaret. *Consensus and Conflict in African Societies*: An Introduction to Sociology. London: Longman, 1977.

Rita, Afsar. "The Conditions and Prospects of Women's Employment in Garment Manufacturing." *Project Overview Gender Programme.* Geneva: Unrisd, 1997.

Chapter 5
Time and the Traditional Palimpsest

Notes

1 Yet another discussion of The Famished Road concerning its post-colonial characteristics is the polemic between Douglass McCabe and Esther De Bruijn. The focal point of their argument is whether Okri's novel has Western modernist elements that are manifest in the form of New Age spirituality (McCabe) or it embodies postcolonial, cosmopolitan text (De Bruijn). See McCabe; De Bruijn for further argument.

2 Murphy also cites Achille Mbembe's comments on the lack of mnemonic traces of slavery in Africa. In his article "African Modes of Self-Writing," Mbembe asserts that "there is, properly speaking, no African memory of slavery" (260).

3 Okri is not alone to theorize an alternative formulation of time. In "Bi-living, Time and Space: LeAnne Howe's Shell Shaker and Chin Ce's The Visitor," Marlene De La Cruze-Guzman argues that authors such as Chin Ce and LeAnne Howe employ coeval realities, or what De La Cruze-Guzman calls "bi-living," that "denotes a rejection of the Western temporal linearity imposed upon the colonized across the world and a privileging of time and space as conceived, perceived, and communicated by indigenous peoples who kept their own sacred,

temporal, spatial assumptions and practices despite superficial acceptance and use of the Western linearity"(75).

4 It is no coincidence that, as Marcus Rediker notes in The Slave Ship: A Human History, the word "spirit" is a terminology used among slave traders, meaning "kidnapping" : "A less common but still-important means of enslavement was trickery, which was used by slave traders to prey upon the naïve and unsuspecting. Among European sailors and indentured servants, the wily labor agent was called a 'spirit,' the process itself 'spiriting' or alternately trepanning or kidnapping" (104).

5 See Murphy's essay for further discussion on the use of a sack to capture slaves. In her essay Murphy argues that the bondage in a bag represents the complete subordination of the African body in slavery. The prime example of this is, Murphy asserts, the classical slave narrative by Olaudah Equiano, when the narrator accounts how he is captured in Benin and shipped to England (Equiano 48). Equiano describes his experience of being put into a sack by his captors so that he is not able to call for help.

Works Cited

Alexander, M. Jacqui. Pedagogies of Crossing: Meditations on Feminism, Sexual Politics, Memory, and the Sacred. Durham and London: Duke University Press, 2005.

Boyce-Davies, Carole. Black Women, Writing and Identity: Migrations of the Subject. London: Routledge, 1994.

De Bruijn, Esther. "Coming to Terms with New Ageist Contamination: Cosmopolitanism in Ben Okri's *The Famished Road.*" *Research in African Literatures* 38:4 (2007): 170-186.

De La Cruze-Guzman, Marlene. "Bi-living, Time and Space: LeAnne Howe's *Shell Shaker* and Chin Ce's *The Visitor.*" *Journal of African Literature and Culture* 7 (2010): 75-88.

Equiano, Olaudah. "The Interesting Narrative of the Life of Olaudah Equiano, or Gustavus Vassa, the African, Written by Himself." 1814. *The Classic Slave Narratives*. Ed. Henry Louis Gates Jr. New York: Signet Classics, 2002, 15-249.

Hartman, Saidiya. *Lose Your Mother: A Journey along the Atlantic Slave Route*. New York: Farrar, Straus and Giroux, 2007.

Hawley, John C. "Ben Okri's Spirit-Child: 'Abiku' Migration and Postmodernity." *Research in African Literatures* 26:1 (1995): 30-39.

Jacobs, Harriet A. *Incident in the Life of a Slave Girl*. 1861. New York: Cosimo, Inc., 2009.

Jewsiewicki Bogumi. and V.Y. Mudimbe. "Africans' Memories and Contemporary History of Africa." *History and Theory* 32:4 (1993):1-11.

Mbembe, Achille. "African Modes of Self-Writing." *Public Culture* 14:1 (2002): 239-73.

McCabe, Douglass. "New Age Spirituality in Ben Okri's *The Famished Road*." *Research in African Literatures* 36:4 (2005): 1-21.

Murphy, Laura. "Into the Bush of Ghosts: Specters of the Slave Trade in West African Fiction." *Research in African Literatures* 38:4 (2007): 141-152.

Ogunsanwo, Olatubosun. "Intertextuality and Post-Colonial Literature in Ben Okri's *The Famished Road*." *Research in African Literatures* 26:1 (1995): 40-52.

Okri, Ben. *The Famished Road*. New York: Nan A. Talese, 1991.

Rediker, Marcus. *The Slave Ship: A Human History*. London and New York: Penguin Books, 2007.

Chapter 6
Poetics of African Naming

Notes

1This refers to the character Kamiti who disguises as soothsayer under the eponymous name Wizard of the Crow to hoodwink the policeman Arigaigai Gathere.

2The name Karega means rebel in Kikuyu. He is a key character in Ngugi's Petals of Blood.

3The Wizard of the Crow therefore becomes an ambiguous name. It represents both Kamiti and Nyawira since she plays the role when Kamiti is away.

4The morphology of this name can also be likened to the 3rd person future tense of the Spanish verb "aburrirse"- to be bored. It could signify the exasperation of life under the dictatorship of a single leader. Many of the names in the text bear Spanish nomenclature (Santalucia church, Santa-Maria police station), which could be influenced by Ngugi's current residence in Hispanic, dominated Irvine, California.

5The capitalized element represents the one with the greatest explanatory force, a decisive factor that affects the other elements of the paradigm.

6Probable pun on Smith Hempstone, US ambassador to Kenya who was very vocal in condemning the atrocities of Daniel Arap Moi and literally arm-twisted the latter into adopting multipartyism. See GBN Ayittey's Africa Betrayed (p.350)

7[L'Etat postcolonial] Prétend détenir la vérité au sujet de la façon de nommer africain et son histoire, de le codifier, de découper l'espace, de l'unifier ou de le diviser. L'Etat-théologien, c'est l'Etat qui ne se préoccupe pas seulement des pratiques touchant á la distribution du pouvoir et de l'influence, aux relations sociales, aux arrangements économiques et aux processus politiques. Il se constitue comme le principe instituant des langages et des mythes d'une société (Mbembe1988 128)

Works Cited

Althusser, Louis. "From Ideology and Ideological State Apparatus" (Notes towards an Investigation) 1970. Vincent B. Leitch et al. *The Norton Anthology of Theory and Criticism*. 2nd Edition. New York: WW Norton and Company, Inc, 2010.

Ayittey, George B N. *Africa Betrayed*. New York: Palgrave Macmillan, 1993.

Bakhtin, Mikhail. *Rabelais and His World*. Bloomington: Indiana University Press, 1984.

Débord, Guy. *Society of the Spectacle*. Detroit: Black and Red, 1983.

Fanon, Frantz. *Black Skin White Masks*. New York: Gerove Weidenfeld, 1967.

Mbembe, Achille. *Afriques Indociles. Christianisme, Pouvoir et Etat en société postcoloniale*. Paris: Karthala 1988.

Nazareth, Peter. "Introduction: Saint Ngugi." *Critical Essays on Ngugi wa Thiong'o*. Ed. Peter Nazareth, New York: Wayne Publishers, 2000. 1-16.

Ngugi wa Thiong'o. *Decolonizing the Mind: The Politics of Language in African Literature*. London: Heinemann, 1986.

_ _ _*Petals of Blood*. London: Heinemann, 1977.

_ _ _. *Wizard of the Crow*. New York: Havil Sacker, 2006.

Ricoeur, Paul. *Time and Narrative*. Vol. 2. Trans. Kathleen McLaughlin and David Pellauer. Chicago and London: University of Chicago Press, 1985.

Said, Edward. *The World, the Text and the Critic*. New York: Faber and Faber, 1984.

White, Hayden. "The Historical Text as a Literary Artifact." *The Norton Anthology of Theory and Criticism*. Ed. Vincent B. Leitch et al. 2nd Edition. New York: WW Norton and Company, Inc, 2010.

Chapter 7
Proverbs in Ojaide's Contexts

Works Cited

Abrams, Peter. *A Glossary of Literary Terms*. 7th ed. Harcourt Brace, 2003.

Achebe, Chinua. *Things Fall Apart*. London: Heinemann, 1958.

Akporobaro, F.B.O. *An Introduction to Oral Literature*. Ikeja: Lighthouse, 2001.

Arora, L. Shirley. "The Perception of Proverbiality." *Wise Words: Essays on the Proverbs*. Ed. Wolfgang Mieder. New York: Garland. 1994:3-29.

Bradbury, Nancy Mason. "Transforming Experience into Tradition: Two theories of Proverb Use and Chaucer's Practice." *Journal of Oral Tradition* Feb. 2002: 261-89. Web. June 2012.

Finnegan, Ruth. *Oral Literature in Africa*. Oxford: Oxford UP, 1970.

Honeck, Richard P, and Jon G. Temple. "Proverbs: The Extended Conceptual Base and Great Chain Metaphor Theories." *Metaphor and Symbolic Activity*.9:85-112.

- - -. "Proverbs and the Complete Mind." *Metaphor and Symbolic Activity 11*. 1996:217-32.

Honeck, Richard P. *A Proverb in Mind*. Mahwah. NJ, Erlbaum, 1997.

Jegede, Olutoyin. "Proverbs Speak Louder than Words: A Study of Contents and Structure in Niyi Osundare's Village Voices." *Ife Studies in African Literature and Arts (Isala)*. 6. (2011):1-15.

Lakoff, George and Mark Johnson. *Metaphors We Live By*. Chicago: U of Chicago P, 1980.

- - -. *More than Cool Reason: A Field Guide to Poetic Metaphor*. Chicago: U of Chicago P, 1989.

Mieder, Wolfgang. *Proverbs Are Never Out of Season: Popular Wisdom in the Modern Age.*Oxford: OUP, 1993.

- - -. ed. *Wise Words: Essay on the Proverbs*. New York: Garland, 1994.
- - -. *International Proverb Scholarship: An Annotated Bibliography: Supplement III (1990-2000)* 2001.
- - -. *Proverbs: A Handbook (Greenwood Folklore Handbook)*. Greenwood: Greenwood Press, 2004.
Murphy, M.J. *Understanding Unseens: An Introduction to English Poetry and the English Novel for Overseas Students*. London: George Allen & Urwin, 1972.
Ogunjimi, Bayo, and Abdul Rasheed N'Allah. *Introduction to African Oral Literature*. Ilorin: Uof Ilorin P, 1991.
Ohaeto, Ezenwa. "Rage and Reason: Moral Education in the Poetry of Ojaide and Udechukwu." *Commonwealth* 16.2 (1993): 19-26. Print.
Ojaide, Tanure. "Poetic Imagination In Black Africa." *Poetic Imagination in Black Africa*. Durham: Carolina Academic Press, 1996: 135-143.
- - -. *Matters of the Moment*. Lagos: Malthouse, 2009. Print.
Okuyade, Ogaga. "The Mythography of Ojaide's Poetry." *African Journal of New Poetry*. Ed. G.M.T Emezue. 3 (2004): 24-25.
Olaofioye, Tayo. *Response to Creativity*. San Diego: Beacon, 1998.
- - -. *The Poetry of Tanure Ojaide. A Critical Appraisal*. Lagos: Malthhouse, 2000.
Osani, Dumbi. "The Aesthetics of Proverbs in Nigerian Fiction: D.O. Fagunwa and Chinua Achebe." *Papers in English and Linguistics (PEL)* 9 (2008): 95-109.
Uyoh, Nancy Emuobosa. "Figurative Expressions as Vehicles of Themes in Ojaide's *Matters of the Matters of the Moment*." Project. U of Benin, 2011.

Chapter 8
Igbo Traditional Morality

Works Cited

Achebe, C. *Things Fall Apart*. London: Heinemann Educational Books, 1958.

Amadi, E. *The Concubine*. London: Heinemann Educational Books, 1966.

Arinze, F. A. *Sacrifice in Igbo Religion*. Ibadan: Ibadan University Press, 1970.

Barcalow, E. *Moral Philosophy: Theory and Issues*. Belmont: Wadsworth Publishing, 1994.

Black, H.C. *Black's Law Dictionary*. St. Paul Minnesota: West Publishing, 1979.

Ce, Chin and Charles Smith (ed.) "Prefatory Note." *Journal of African Literature*. No. 9, 2012.

Esomonu, L.E. *Respect for Human Life in Igbo Religion and Morality*. Rome: Tipographica Leberit, 1981.

Ezedike, E.U. "Moral Problems in Nigeria: The Relevance of Traditional Ethics to Contemporary African Society." Ed. A.F.Uduigwomen. *From Footmarks to Landmarks in African Philosophy*. Calabar: Jochrisam Publishers, 2009.

Hart, H.L.A. "Punishment and Responsibility." *Essays in the Philosophy of Law*. Oxford: Clarendon Press, 1980.

Iroegbu, P. Metaphysics: *The Kpim of Philosophy*. Owerri: I.U.P, 1995.

Iwe, N.S.S. *Socio-Ethical Issues in Nigeria*. Oruowulu-Obosi: Pacific Publishers, 1991.

Mbiti, J.S. *African Religions and Philosophy*. London: Heinemann, 1969.

Nduka, O. *Western Education and Nigerian Cultural Background*. Ibadan: Oxford University Press, 1964.

Okere, T. "The Assumption of African Values as Christian Values." *Lucerna*. 1, (July-Dec, 1978) 6-15.

Olong, A.M. *The Nigerian Legal System: An Introduction*. Lagos: Malthouse Press, 2009.

Omoregbe, J. Ethics: *A Systematic and Historical Study*. Lagos: Joja Educational Research and Publishers, 1993.

Otakpo, N. *Justice in Igbo Culture*. Lagos: Malthouse Press, 2009.

Osborne, T. M. "Crime and Punishment of Criminal." Ed. H. S. Spalding. *Social Problems and Agencies*. New York, Beniger Brothers, 1925: 250-271.

Ozumba, G.O. "The Concept of Punishment and African Philosophy." *Unizik Journal of Arts and Humanities*. Vol 1 No 1. 2001.58-63.

Pazhaym-Pallil, T. *Pastoral Guide*. India: Andhra Pradesh, 1977.

Plato. *Laws*. Ed. Hamilton and Cairns, *Collected Dialogues of Plato*. New York: Bantam Books, 2006.

Sterba, J.P. *Morality in Practice*. California: Wadsworth Publishing, 1989.

Thiroux, J.P. *Ethics: Theory and Practice*. California: Glencoe Publishing, 1980.

Vellanga, J. "Christianity and Capital Punishment." *Death Penalty in America*. Ed. H. Bedau. New York: O.U.P, 1952.

Chapter 9
Naming in Esanland

Works Cited

Adler, A. S. *The individual Psychology of Alfred Adler: A Systematic Presentation of His Writings*. 2nd Edition New York: Harper and Row, 1964.

Glasser, W. *Reality Therapy: A New Approach to Psychiatry*. New York: Harper and Row, 1965.

Valfre, Morrison. *Foundations of Mental Health Care.* 3rd Edition. Mosby Inc. 2005.

Trull, T. J and E. J. Phares. *Clinical Psychology.* 6th Edition. Wardsworth: Thomas Learning, 2001.

Waldinger, R. J. *Psychiatry for Medical Students.* Washington: American Psychiatric Press. 1997.

Whitehall, H. et al *Westerner's New Twentieth Dictionary of English Language.* Cleveland: World Publication, 1950.

Gove, P. B., et al. Webster's Third New Internal Dictionary of the English Language. Massachusetts: G.C Merriam Company Publishers, 1971.

Talbot, P. A. *The Peoples of Southern Nigeria Vol. II.* London: Frank Cass and Company, 1969.

Omoregie, J. O. *Edo Names for Cultural Studies.* Benin: New Age Publication, 2000.

Female Subjectivities

SINCE western civilization, women have confronted what they perceive to be male domination of affairs in human society where it had seemed that facets of the society must conform to the male order before they are adjudged to be correct. In literature the ambiguous portraiture of female characters by some male writers and the phallic nature of men's writings have proved a matter of concern to female writers in Africa. For decades within African writing the issue of silencing was interrogated particularly as it addressed the muting and marginalisation of black women by male writers, and the script of patriarchy which they follow.

In this series we continue the literary and dramatic tradition of feminist concern for women's issues and we r˗ novels, plays and poetry wh demonstrate a commitment to ᴄ..ᵣ the challenges facing modern women in changing times and excerpting the issues of gender, feminism, identity, race, history, national and international politics specifically as they affect women. Female Subjectivities collectively answers the need to question and adumbrate the possibilities of literary revisions, showing v ˈ ˙˙˙ would mean to revise even the psychoanalyst in a discourse on the subjectivity of women of colour.

Our Critical Approaches

Chin Ce, African writer from Nigeria, fellow of the Literary Society and author of several books of poetry, critical essays and prose fictions, is editor of the Critical Writing Series on African Literature with Charles Smith, professor of African languages and literature, founder of the Society of African Folklore and fellow of the Literary Society International, LSi.

Our Mission

"Our select projects at African Books Network have given boost to the renaissance of a whole generation of dynamic literature."

African Books Network

AFRICAN Books Network with its cosmopolitan outlook is poised to meet the book needs of African generations in times to come.

Since the year 2000 when we joined the information highway of online solutions in publishing and distribution, our African alliance to global information development excels in spite of challenges in the region. Our select projects have given boost to the renaissance of a whole generation of dynamic literature. In our wake is the harvest of titles that have become important referrals in contemporary literary studies. With print issues followed by eContent and eBook versions, our network has demonstrated its commitment to the vision of a continent bound to a common world heritage. This universal publishing outlook is further evidenced by our participation in African Literature Research projects. For everyone on deck, a hands-on interactive is the deal which continues to translate to more flexibility in line with global trends ensuring that African writers are part of the information revolution of the present times.

As one of Africa's mainstream book publishing and distribution networks, writers may look forward to privileged assistance regarding affiliate international and local publishing and distribution service

www.ingramcontent.com/pod-product-compliance
Lightning Source LLC
Chambersburg PA
CBHW010832230426
43668CB00019BA/2416